# Contents

# *Preface*

About 12 years ago, I purchased my first pair of Musschenbroek's lorikeets (*Neopsittaccus musschenbroekii*). I was attracted not only by the stunning colors of these birds, but also by the fact that this is one of the few lorikeets that will do well on a captive diet of seeds (with fruit and universal food, of course). Though their voices are somewhat strident, they more than make up for this by being relatively easy to house and care for, and their liveliness and somewhat aggressive nature makes them very interesting subjects for the aviary. Since then I have kept many lories and lorikeets in my aviaries, and have also had the opportunity to study them for some time in the wild, especially in Australia and New Guinea.

In recent years, particularly since the beginning of the 1980s, many species of lories and lorikeets have become high in popularity and you may now find them available in many pet stores.

Unfortunately, there is a shortage of good literature available on this group of birds and the only substantial books on the subject (with the exception of the recently published, very comprehensive work *Lories and Lorikeets in Aviculture* by John Vanderhoof) are very much out-of-date. The only other English language book of any substance (recently republished but not revised) is Rosemary Low's book (see Bibliography, page 89) and that is more than 15 years old.

I am thus very glad to have prepared this book about the "brush-tongued parrots"—the lories and the lorikeets. I am especially pleased to offer my advice, as most bird fanciers do not realize what they are getting themselves into when they acquire specimens of these birds. They may know that most of them have a staple diet of nectar and fruit (but may still try to see how long they will survive on a seed diet!) and that they are rather messy birds (as are most fruit eaters). In spite of what you may have read in popular bird magazines, lories and lorikeets can NOT live on a staple diet of seeds, especially dry, hard ones! Un-fortunately, many captive lories and lorikeets are still fed on seeds alone and these birds, though possibly surviving for several torturous years, eventually will die from malnutrition!

I have specially researched the material for this book and have consulted top breeders in Europe, Australia, and the United States. However, do not expect this to be a strictly scientific text—I have endeavored to produce an interesting, readable work that is comprehensible to every fancier.

I wish to thank the following friends and aviculturists who, in one way or another, have helped me in the preparation of this work. These include Drs. Alice DeGroot, MSc, DVM; Petra Burgmann, DVM; Amy Vansonnenberg, DVM; and Steven Wehrmann, DVM (all of the United States or Canada); Drs. P. E. Roders, DVM; G.T. Kaal, DVM, and S. Tol, DVM (all of the Netherlands); the late Remi Ceuleers, and Paula Leysen (Belgium), and Theo Pagel (Germany). My heartfelt thanks go also to my friend, the biologist John Coborn (Australia), for the work he has taken off my hands, and my friend and editor at Barron's, Don Reis. A special acknowledgment must go to my wife, Lucia Vriends-Parent, for her positive support, assistance, and continued unselfish encouragement in my work. Last but not least, I thank my dear friend, Kathy Egbert, who assisted me in the many laboratory experiments related to feeding.

Any observations or constructive criticism that can improve the text should be communicated via the publisher so that such improvements can be included in any reprinting.

Matthew M. Vriends
Loveland, Ohio
Fall, 1992
*Soyons fidèles à nos faiblesses.*
For Victor Schmelzer, MD and Donald L. Wayne, MD–in gratitude and friendship.

# *Considerations Before Purchasing*

Lories and lorikeets are definitely not for everybody. However, the fact that they are now much easier to feed (a task that took up a great deal of time in the past) thanks to the various excellent commercial foods that are available (see page 25), brings these colorful, acrobatic, and intelligent birds within the reach of any fancier who wishes to own them. In general, these birds do not require a great deal of aviary space and they soon become tame and affectionate toward their owner.

Lories and lorikeets are relatively more expensive than other birds, and, due to their great popularity, poor quality birds often are offered on the market. Beginners, especially, soon can become disillusioned when, after spending a lot of money, they find themselves a few days later with dead or sick birds. Lories and lorikeets also must be kept in single pairs and never together with other species of parrotlike birds; thus if you want a collection of birds, you must have several aviaries. This is also not cheap. (Before constructing aviaries you must first discuss matters with your family and neighbors, bearing in mind that lories and lorikeets are noisy birds, especially if disturbed by a skulking cat, or if you go too close to a nest box when they have eggs or nestlings.)

Lorikeets require special, time-consuming care; especially with regard to aspects of hygiene. It is important to have well-constructed aviaries with concrete floors and drainage. If aviaries are to be constructed indoors, it is best to have the floor covered with washable ceramic or terracotta tiles (see page 20). All aviaries also must be outfitted with misting devices (see page 21).

Although there are some species that learn to repeat words very well, for example the dusky lory (*Pseudeos f. fuscata*) and various *Lorius* and *Eos* species, and others that are not difficult to tame and make into excellent "pets," for example, Duivenbode's lory (*Chalcopsitta d. duivenbodei*), most lories and lorikeets are unsuitable for cages or as pet birds! They are much too active and (I have to say with all honesty) too messy. Pieces of fruit are scattered left and right over the furniture and the fluid droppings are literally squirted out of the cage onto the carpet!

Of course, you don't acquire your first birds until your quarantine aviary is complete and you are quite clear about the required diet. If the birds are feeding on a menu different than what you had planned, carry on with the "bad" diet to which they are accustomed and gradually change it to your new one over a week or so. To detect possible internal parasites it is advisable to have the droppings of newly acquired birds examined at a veterinary laboratory. New birds are best kept separately or, if there is too little space, in pairs. During the month of quarantine, the birds must be observed closely and under no circumstances allowed to come into contact with any of your existing stock. Only after thorough acclimatization and veterinary clearance, should they join the main collection.

## Where to Buy Lories and Lorikeets

It should be quite obvious that your birds are preferably obtained from a reputable breeder or dealer. If you do not know any supplier, maybe your avian veterinarian, or the manager of your local pet store will know a supplier. In the fall (usually), in most urban areas, there are often many kinds of bird shows in which all types of birds are exhibited. Here you will undoubtedly get contacts or even discover the best breeders; these will be the ones that have won first prizes in the lory and lorikeet sections! And another tip: join a bird society! Do not be afraid to ask questions.

Beginners to the hobby already may have some ideas about the good and bad points of their prospective purchases, but it is still best to get the help of an experienced fancier. An alert bird keeper can tell if the bird is in the best of health and sometimes whether it is a cock or hen. The experienced fancier will be able to discover any

# *Considerations Before Purchasing*

signs of disability or ailments and comment on the good and bad points of a bird. Whether you get experienced advice, or rely on your own instincts, you should not restrict your attention just to the birds.

The condition of the establishment holding the birds is as important as the birds themselves. If the place is full of dirty, smelly, overcrowded cages; if it is cluttered and untidy; and if the proprietor's attitude leaves much to be desired— then it is best to go elsewhere.

It always pays to go yourself to purchase birds. If at all possible, never order birds on the telephone or by mail order, collect them in person. You are dealing with living beings, with feelings and demands, not inanimate pieces of furniture!

## What to Look For

Always try to get young stock, but preferably birds successfully through their first molt. Obtain as much information as you can about the parents of the birds, and ask for details of feeding schedules and breeding habits. It is important to know what kind of nest box the birds were reared in, so that you can offer a similar nest box for them to breed in. Research has shown that breeding pairs are strongly attracted to similar nest boxes to those in which they came into the world. Take note of all these points and any changes you wish to make must be made gradually over a period of several weeks.

Newly imported birds that come into your hands via quarantine, obviously must be treated with the greatest of care. Diet and temperature are very important. Feed exactly what the birds have been eating already and change over to a new diet very gradually over 8 to 12 days. If possible, isolate each new bird in a roomy cage or (better still) an inside aviary and keep at a minimum of room temperature. Provide the newcomers with luke-

warm water to bathe in. Collect fecal samples and get them off to your veterinarian as soon as possible, making sure you know which samples came from which birds! (Once the bird is settled, it can be examined by an avian veterinarian who will inspect the mucus membranes inside the mouth and nostrils for signs of infection.) Inspect the feet to make sure they are not misformed and that all four toes are complete. Toeless birds often have difficulties when it comes to mating because they cannot maintain a good grip!

It is important to get a written guarantee that a bird will be exchanged if it does not turn out to be the sex it is supposed to be. The sexes of lories and lorikeets can be determined by DNA-blood or endoscopic examination (see page 31); before buying a bird, it may be worth having it sexed this way (often the cost of sexing is included in the price).

Imported birds often have had their wings pinioned, or the flight feathers of one or both wings clipped. Pinioned birds should not be purchased. Birds with clipped flight feathers are another matter however; these will be fully feathered again after the next satisfactory molt. For the time being, they will have to be content with clambering about the perches and on the cage wire. You can help them by providing extra perches during this period and do not forget to provide a "pathway to the nest box," which, outside the breeding season, is also used as a bedroom.

Wherever they come from, birds with no flesh on the breast and with the breastbone sticking out sharply, should really never be purchased. Such birds will have been half starved over a protracted period or suffer fron chronic diseases, e.g., tuberculosis or aspergillosis; and experience has shown that it is extremely difficult to get them back into reasonable condition (although of course one is to be commended for trying!). A bit of love and dedication can sometimes work wonders! And I can guarantee that one of the greatest joys a fancier can have is to bring such a bird back to health and give it the love of life again.

Prospective purchasers often stand right next to the cages when observing birds. Of course they want to get a close look at the birds before making a decision. But it is also a good idea to view the birds from a moderate distance when they are in their display cages.

When you approach closely, healthy birds are likely to show fear by taking flight but still keeping an eye on you as a possible threat. A sick bird may walk or fly away, but the more sick it is the less notice it will take of you. Do not think a bird is tame because it doesn't fly away; it is more likely to be sick. Therefore, purchase only those birds that are alert, agile, and observant.

Lories and lorikeets can give rather severe nips with their powerful beaks, so it is wise to wear strong gloves when handling them. A manual examination before purchase, however, is very advisable. Take the bird in the gloved hand and examine it from beak to tail tip. The beak should close properly and the surface should be smooth. Make sure there are no bald patches on top of the head, and that the wing and tail feathers are not damaged. Look at the feet one at a time; they should be clean and smooth and, as mentioned earlier, with a complete set of toes and claws. In old birds, you may see calcium deposits on the claws.

Feel the flesh on either side of the breastbone that runs down the center of the breast. It should be firm and plump, not hollow with the breastbone showing through like a blade.

Examine the area around the vent. If this is dirty, matted, and/or stained, it probably means the bird has some kind of intestinal disorder and therefore, obviously should *not* be purchased.

Hold the bird close to your ear (watch your ear!) and listen to its breathing. A squeaking, grating, or gasping noise could mean it has a respiratory infection and should not be purchased.

A sick bird will be dull-eyed and also probably have its eyes partly closed. Sometimes it sticks its head into its plumage or under its wing and fluffs its feathers right out. The wings are often droopy and the body position is more horizontal than vertical. Sometimes the bird will come close to falling off its perch. The bird will not sing or call and will take little, if any, food. If it does try to eat, it probably will waste more than it swallows. There may be a nasal discharge or even vomiting or regurgitating. The latter is the process by which the bird voluntarily brings food (seeds and other eaten materials) and some mucus up from the crop in order to feed another bird, or to welcome its owner; vomiting is an involuntary process in which the bird brings up mucus and a little food.

Blow gently on the breast feathers so that they part and you can see the skin, which should be clean and healthy, not red and spotty.

Based on the preceding criteria, you can be fairly sure of getting a healthy bird. Of course, it is not suggested that any of the symptoms described are necessarily fatal to lories and lorikeets. There are treatments for these and other ailments, but you obviously will not want to be plagued with such problems right from the beginning.

The best advice can be summarized in a dozen words: never buy inferior material; buy the best and healthiest you can afford!

## When to Buy Lories and Lorikeets

It is always best to acquire any aviary birds during the warmer parts of the year, that is late spring to early fall when the difference between indoor and outdoor temperatures is not too great. During late spring and summer, however, you may find lories and lorikeets to be in short supply as most birds are being used for breeding. Any birds you do see offered for sale are likely to be weak or substandard specimens that have been rejected for breeding purposes. If possible, therefore, try to purchase birds in the early fall; the temperature should not yet be too great a problem and you will have the greatest choice of the current season's youngsters.

## Transporting Lories and Lorikeets

Lories and lorikeets should not be transported in large, ornamental cages. Even if such a cage was wrapped in some sort of covering, the frightened bird would probably flap about and injure itself. A traumatic journey also will make a bird nervous and exhausted, not a good start in its new home. All birds therefore should be carried in special traveling boxes. Most avicultural dealers supply stout, ventilated, cardboard boxes in various sizes so that a bird can sit comfortably, some-

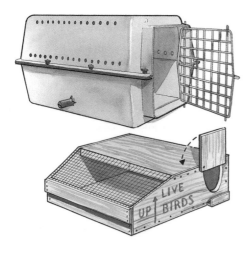

Top: A plastic kennel/carrier. There are many models available. They should have a two- or four- pronged locking mechanism on the door for security. Owners should place the carrier on the floor and allow the bird to check it out. The carrier's floor should be lined with brown wrapping paper. A substantial fruit dish must be provided.
Bottom: A sturdy shipping container. Always check first with airlines or other carriers about their rules and regulations. The crate must be large enough to allow the bird to stand up and turn around.

what restrained but with enough space for it to move about without injuring itself.

Of course, cardboard boxes are only suitable for relatively short journeys and rarely can be used more than two or three times as the birds are likely to start chewing at them with their powerful beaks. If you intend to do a lot of lory or lorikeet transporting, or for your annual visits to the veterinarian, you will require a more substantial transport box. Such a box can be made from wood, an ideal size being about 12 by 10 by 10 inches (30 x 25 x 25 cm), with a fine wire mesh front. Whatever kind of traveling case you use, make sure the ventilation holes are not blocked with wrapping materials, labels, or similar items.

Adequate food (fruits and greens) for the journey should be strewn on the floor of the transport box and, if you have to make a long journey, a little moist bread will supply the necessary water. Do not be concerned that the bird will be unable to find food in the darkness of the cage. During various study trips to Australia, my wife and I regularly observed lories and lorikeets as well as cockatiels, budgerigars, rosellas, cockatoos, and other birds foraging for food in the evenings and even at night by weak moonlight (see page 18). Our aviary birds also regularly feed late into dusk.

## Welcome Home!

When you arrive home with a new bird you must first make sure all doors, windows, and similar openings are secure, that there are no unguarded open fires, and that all gas or electric appliances are switched off in case a bird should escape. If all is in order, the bird may be trans-

Top: The black-winged lory, known for its strong musky odor.
Bottom left: The red lory is the most popular member of its genus.
Bottom right: During the night the violet-necked lory roosts in a nest box.

ferred from its traveling case to its new home, preferably a quarantine cage or aviary. This may be done simply by placing the open doors of each cage together and allowing the bird to move itself. After a little hesitation most birds will move without too much prompting, but it may be necessary to help the occasional bird along by gently guiding it with your hand.

Mornings are the best time to install birds into their new accommodations; certainly before noon, so that there is time to adjust to the strange surroundings before darkness sets in. A bird will thus have time to orient itself with regard to perches, nest boxes, and other furnishings and to select a comfortable roosting spot for the night. A bird placed in new surroundings late in the day may remain nervous and restless all night, possibly injuring itself.

Many newly acquired birds are young or recently imported and will have come from large stock aviaries or flights, often together with many other (non-psittacine) birds. Others may come from the well-known barred parrot cages and will thus be accustomed to certain types of food and water containers. After introducing a new bird to your premises, stand back and observe it quietly to make sure that it finds its new food hopper. In case of doubt place a number of food dishes at various heights, including some on platforms about 18 inches (45 cm) from the floor. Lories and lorikeets are always hungry so it should not take them long to find their food. New food containers may not be accepted immediately; however, the birds will start to "experiment" once

Top left: A rather young yellow-streaked lory and (bottom) its parents.
Top right: The Duivenbode's lory is an excellent pet!

driven by the urge of hunger. To be on the safe side, you can also strew a little fruit and green food about various parts of the aviary.

## Handling Your New Bird

In general, it is advisable not to handle newly acquired birds at all if possible. They should have been inspected at the dealer's premises and this, coupled with the journey home, already will have placed some strain on them. Most birds hate being gripped and it often will cause them temporary stress, even shock. However, there are always times when it becomes necessary to catch a bird and remove it from its home. If your catching technique is too rough, there is a chance the bird will be injured and, conversely, if you take too much time doing it, the bird will become exhausted and distressed.

I remember well my first Duivenbode's lories, which I had received by air freight via Miami. Unsuspectingly, I stuck my unprotected hand into the traveling cage and was immediately viciously attacked by one of the birds. I withdrew my hand quickly of course, but the feisty little bird hung on to my little finger as the blood streamed over my hand. I had to get the bird off but it just wouldn't let go! Over the years I have developed a great respect for the sharp beaks of my colorful friends the lories! Their beaks are efficient weapons that are used with little provocation when they feel insecure. Once accustomed to their new accommodations, and keeper, however, they quickly become tame and trusting, due to their fearless nature and profound curiosity.

A lory or lorikeet is best caught in flight, not while it hangs on the cage or aviary wire as it will not relax its powerful grip. It is useless to try to "loosen" the toes from the wire as you cannot re-

11

lease the toes without injuring the bird. Always use a padded net with a relatively short handle. The right time to catch a lory or lorikeet in the hand is when it sits on the floor. You should wear strong gloves. If I need to catch a lory or lorikeet just to move it to another cage or aviary, I use the bird's natural behavior to advantage. In aviaries, the birds will disappear rapidly into their nest boxes—which they also use as a "bedroom"—when you enter. Take down the nest box with the bird inside and hold the entrance hole against the door of the cage or whatever and coax the bird out into its new home.

Untame lories and lorikeets, especially the larger species, can be very upset by the use of a net. Tame birds can be taken from one place to another on your arm or shoulder but untrained birds don't want to know anything about nets; as soon as they realize what you are about to do, they will make for the nest box.

Sometimes a bird will lay on the ground on its back and kick its legs. It should be quickly caught in a net, then transferred to a transport box before being taken to its new accommodation. Work quickly, resolutely, and effectively; that is the best for both you and the birds.

# *Understanding Lories and Lorikeets*

## Introduction

During the last few years, lories and lorikeets have experienced a well-deserved increase in popularity among aviculturists. With their clown-like behavior and their brilliant colors, they are truly a feast for the eyes and excellent subjects for aviaries and (for some species) for large cages. In the past, fanciers regarded these birds with perhaps less enthusiasm than they might, due to their specialized diet and the fact that their droppings are watery and messy, which meant that cages had to be cleaned thoroughly on a daily basis.

## Geographical Notes

The "heart" of "lory country" is Australasia, but especially New Guinea and its tiny eastern islands, which include the last "lory strongholds" of Henderson Island and the little Pitcairn Ducie Islands, where in 1907, the Stephen's lory (*Vini stephensi*) was discovered. This bird is now rarely if ever seen in captivity, though I once viewed a specimen owned by a Belgian fancier. I am not aware of any American specimens. Traveling westward from New Guinea, the many islands of Indonesia are located, all populated with lories as far as Bali and Lombok where the Mitchell's lorikeet (*Trichoglossus haematodus mitchelli*) is found. This is a splendid bird with a light red breast, which appears irregularly on the market.

Some of the lory species from Henderson Island to Bali have a surprisingly large range and several occur on two or more islands. The climate and availability of food may have some bearing on the distribution of various subspecies. The well-known German ornithologist Dr. H. E. Wolters would recognize 56 species, though I would be doubtful about three of these; another one, the New Caledonian lorikeet (*Hypocharmosyna diadema*), is probably extinct. Of the 134 subspecies recognized by Dr. Wolters, there are at least 15 that can be regarded as synonyms of the nominate forms or at least with doubtful status.

Personally, I do not believe it is necessary to give subspecies status on account of small color differences; all lories and lorikeets (with a few exceptions) possess a varied color pattern that easily could lead to mistaken classifications. I am of the opinion that further studies based on morphological rather than color characteristics are necessary before any hard and fast ornithological decisions can be made regarding the classifications of this group of species.

## Nutrition

The main diet of lories and lorikeets is the nectar of flowering trees, but much pollen also is devoured as well as sweet, soft fruits and berries; sometimes the soft, unripe seeds of grass and other plants are also eaten. Insects and their larvae are taken eagerly at all times, but especially during the breeding season. All lories and lorikeets I have ever kept have been crazy about maggots, mealworms (which for safety's sake are first soaked for a few minutes in boiling water), and ant pupae. Flocks of wild lories can be a nuisance in orchards where they will damage much unripe fruit in search of their sweet and ripe favorites. In Indonesia, I have seen apple and pear harvests totally destroyed by hundreds of these birds. I also have seen corn, sorghum, and wheat crops severely damaged. The local people try to keep the birds away with empty food cans suspended on strings so that they bang together in the breeze and create a frightful noise; if this doesn't work then, unfortunately, the guns come out!

In view of their preferred diet, and due to the fact that lories and lorikeets nest high up in hol-

# Understanding Lories and Lorikeets

low limbs and trunks of mainly eucalyptus trees, it seems fairly obvious that most of the birds inhabit fairly thickly wooded areas, even high into montane forest. Some species are quite nomadic and follow the flowering of the food trees; some of them frequently cover fair distances from island to island. Indeed most lories and lorikeets are very adept fliers, recognized by their straight and fast flight. Many of them travel around in fairly large flocks so that they are protected against hawks and other predators that seem to prefer single birds as prey. Once, in the Celebes, I observed a flock of ornate lorikeets (*Trichoglossus ornatus*). Suddenly a few birds, obviously in fear, separated from the main flock as they were pursued by a hawk. The hawk flew between the main flock and the separated birds and, with a swoop, took the most isolated bird in its talons before making off.

Lories are very cautious and will fly quickly, shrilling constantly while over open tracts of land. They become calmer when back among the trees, but always remain alert. Should a flock of lorikeets be pursued by a bird of prey—which does not happen very often—the birds will attempt to remain grouped and will make for the nearest stand of trees. Once there, they quickly seek refuge among the foliage where few birds of prey will pursue them. Do not imagine that once the birds have taken refuge, they will sit still and remain silent. They soon will return to their lively, clownlike and quarrelsome foraging as if nothing had happened; especially if they had been lucky enough to land amidst blossoming trees! It is indeed a wonderful sight to experience a flock of lories foraging among their food trees. Sometimes they are in company with several other nectar and pollen eating bird species; in general they tolerate each other and interspecific aggression is rarely observed.

If individual flocks should come together, one will really experience how lively and vocal these birds are; they never forgo their lively behavior even in a roomy aviary.

Lories and lorikeets use all manner of actions to reach their food; twisting, squirming, and hanging, often suspended by one foot in order to reach an elusive bloom. It is interesting to observe that a particular group of lories will accept a lost or stray member of their own species without problems but, in times of food shortages, they may attempt to drive off other species, though they do not always get the upper hand. In this connection, it is paradoxical that excited lories at a food source actually will attract other blossom feeding species with their constant chatter and thus have to share. Other groups of lories also may be attracted and, in such cases there is seldom protest and the birds will feed together in harmony.

When a flock of lories or lorikeets discovers a suitable flowering tree, the birds first land in the upper foliage and look carefully around to make sure the coast is clear. If all is well, they then begin to forage. A second group of lories landing in the same tree will behave in exactly the same wary manner, even if the first group is already busy foraging. Should there be a sudden disturbance, the whole (or both) flock(s) will rise "as one bird" and fly screechingly away. Should it be a false alarm, the birds soon will return to the tree and forage again, after making a couple of cautionary circuits around the area. If real danger should threaten, then the flock will fly off to a more thickly wooded area where it will feel safer.

Of course, there are also dangers during the breeding period and, should danger threaten, the whole group will leave the nesting tree and return only when the coast is clear. The incubating or brooding hens return first to their nests. When there is no immediate danger, the breeding cocks will feed the incubating hens three or four times a day. Even when there are young in the nest they will keep up a similar pattern, once in the morning, twice during the day, and once more towards evening, feeding both their mate and the young.

# *Understanding Lories and Lorikeets*

## Breeding Behavior

Wild lories and lorikeets breed in the hollow limbs and trunks of trees. The entrance hole may be enlarged and the interior of the nest is usually intensively modified by gnawing. This results in a soft layer of wood pulp in the base of the hollow, which often is supplemented by the birds with a few eucalyptus leaves to make a bed for the eggs. A few species, but especially those in the genus *Vini*, occasionally may use the hollowed out interior of a rotten coconut to raise their offspring. With most species the hen lays two, but occasionally three or more, white, round-oval eggs. The eggs are incubated by the hen without direct assistance from her mate but the cock frequently relieves her for a few minutes. It is unfortunately not clear if the cock actually sits on the eggs during these periods. I have had the opportunity of examinining wild, breeding lories on several occasions and I have never found brooding patches on males. The cock also, usually, spends the night in the nest hollow with the hen, but I have not been able to ascertain if the cock is, or is not, actually involved with the incubation of the eggs.

The smaller species have an incubation period of 17 to 23 days, the medium-sized species about 25 days, and the largest species up to 30 days. At hatching time, the youngsters are covered with a thick white layer of down, which becomes gray after a few days. In just a few weeks they gain their feathers, and when they leave the nest they are so well feathered that they are difficult to distinguish from their parents. For the first weeks the youngsters continue to use their nest hollow at night, but after two or three weeks they become more or less independent, leave their parents, and join up with the general flock. If it is a good year and there is plenty of food available, a second brood may be started shortly after the first has fledged. In really good years, even three broods may be reared.

Pairs of lorikeets become very aggressive during breeding and will not tolerate any interference. Birds that approach too close to the nest will be vigorously repelled and, in serious cases, blood may flow! They also will vigorously defend the nest against such egg or nestling predators as monkeys or tree martens; however, with felines, snakes, and other large reptiles, courage is lost and the birds will retire protestingly and noisily to a nearby tree. Some of the most serious predators are rats, which have been introduced to many islands by human activities. Isolated species with a small range of habitat are especially vulnerable to or endangered by such predation, including many from the genera *Vini* and *Phigys*. The greatest danger of all, ironically perhaps, is human exploitation of the land. Clearing, draining, reclamation, deforestation, industry, and agriculture have all contributed to the serious demise of many species. One serious problem is loss of nesting sites. It takes many years for eucalyptus trees (the main nesting trees of many species in Indonesia and Australia) to age sufficiently to have large enough hollow limbs for nesting. If all the old trees are cleared, there is a shortage of nesting sites. Cleared areas may be developed for many uses but, even if they were reforested with eucalyptus trees, it would be at least a hundred years before they were again suitable for hole nesters.

## Water

During my observations of wild populations, it became obvious to me that lories and lorikeets do not readily leave their feeding or breeding tree (often one and the same tree), even to go drinking or bathing. If they should have a choice, they would rather drink from the early morning dew, or raindrops on the leaves of the tree. To bathe they use the rain, or frolic among the dew soaked foliage, rather than leave their beloved tree. As they take mainly moist food, drinking water is rela-

# *Understanding Lories and Lorikeets*

tively unimportant to lories and lorikeets when compared with seed eating birds, but they still must always have a fresh supply in their cage or aviary. Some species, especially those in the genus *Trichoglossus*, occasionally fly to a stream or slow flowing river and more or less do a "belly flop" on the water surface with their wings spread before flying to a nearby perch to complete their grooming. Captive specimens also appreciate facilities for taking a bath and if you offer them a shallow dish of clean water they most likely will frolic in the water with obvious enjoyment.

## Some Ornithological Facts

J. Forshaw (1973) recognizes 11 genera, 55 species, and 88 subspecies in the subfamily Lorinae. J. L. Peters (1937) recognized 15 genera, whereas Dr. H. E. Wolters (1982) believes the figures to be 13 genera, 56 species, and 134 subspecies (see also page 13). Whoever may be right is immaterial; a compromising view must be taken. What is more important is that interest be maintained in the birds themselves. Enthusiasm for the group had already started in London in 1774 when the first illustrations of these birds arrived from Australia. Soon the fantastic colors and patterns were the talk of the scientific world. Interestingly, the whole color spectrum may be found in the plumage of lories and lorikeets: melanin (black, gray, brown), carotenoid (especially yellow, orange, and red), and the structure color blue (and violet). There are also uniformly colored species, the black lorikeet (*Chalopsittaatra*), for example, and various species in the genus *Charmosyna*, the so-called ornamental lories.

Most species have 12 tail feathers, but beautiful mountain lories (*Oreopsittacus*) have 14. The genera *Phigys* (solitory lories) and *Vini* (virgin lories) have extended neck feathers that they can puff out when excited or during courtship. The wings are relatively long, the tail short to me-

dium, sometimes with a pair of extended middle tail feathers. The beak is somewhat narrow and elongated.

One of the most important lory characteristics is the brush-tipped tongue, which is quite long and narrow. At the tongue tip, there are several rows of papillae arranged in a U formation. During feeding, the papillae are erected, so that pollen and nectar can be brushed from the food flow-

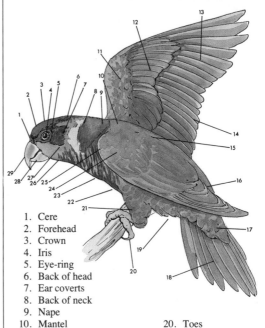

1. Cere
2. Forehead
3. Crown
4. Iris
5. Eye-ring
6. Back of head
7. Ear coverts
8. Back of neck
9. Nape
10. Mantel
11. Middle and lesser coverts
12. Primary coverts
13. Primaries
14. Secondaries
15. Back
16. Rump
17. Uppertail coverts
18. Tail coverts
19. Undertail coverts
20. Toes
21. Thigh
22. Abdomen
23. Breast
24. Shoulder
25. Band of wing
26. Chin
27. Cheek
28. Lower mandible
29. Upper mandible

Knowing the various parts of the body is especially useful when talking with your avian veterinarian.

# Understanding Lories and Lorikeets

Lories and lorikeets are known as "brush-tongued parrots" because of their unique tongues that are used to lap up the flower nectar, pollen, plant buds and insects.

ers. Once loaded with pollen, the tongue is withdrawn into the mouth and the brush scraped across a fold of skin on the palate so that the food is removed. The tongue papillae are of various lengths depending on the species and it can safely be said that the more dependent the species is on pollen and nectar, the longer the tongue papillae will be. This is particularly evident in the genera *Phigys*, *Vini*, *Charmosyna*, and *Hypochyarmosyna*. A colleague, Pagel, has observed for example that the Johnstone's lorikeet (*Trichoglossus j. johnstoneiae*) from the island of Mindanao (Philippines) and the Iris lory (*Trichoglossus* or *Glossopsitta i. iris*) from western Timor have relatively short papillae, which shows that seeds are a large part of the birds' diets; not hard, dry seeds as obtained on the market, but soft unripe seeds. The base of the tongue is not only a

support for the relatively long tongue itself but also assists in the erection of the papillae. The papillae erect automatically as the tongue is extended.

With reference to the fold of skin on the palate mentioned previously, it is interesting to note that many ornithologists use this as a major taxonomical characteristic in bird classification. For example, the palate-fold in the Iris lory is situated much further back in the mouth than in the genera *Phigys*, *Vini*, *Charmosyna*, and *Hypocharmosyna* where it is situated more in the middle of the palate. It should not be forgotten that lories and lorikeets play a major role in the pollination of many flowering trees and other plants.

Most of the lories and lorikeets have poorly developed gizzards and thus find it difficult to satisfactorily process dry, hard seeds. However, it is interesting to see how a lory or lorikeet de-husks seeds with the edges of its mandibles. In the wild, half-ripe seed is also thus treated and the tongue is used to move the seed into the ideal positions. Seeds are not swallowed whole or merely crushed, but de-husked, a trait characteristic of all psittacines. Large seeds are frequently held in one of the feet.

Fruits are first cautiously tested with the tip of the tongue before the point of the upper mandible bites into the flesh, while the edge of the lower mandible completes the biting process. A piece of fruit flesh is then manipulated with the tongue, while the mandibles make a sort of chewing motion with the fruit being pressed against the horny palate. The juices that are pressed out are swallowed, while any unused debris such as pips or skin are thrown out with a shake of the head. It is therefore useful to have cages lined with plastic so that they can easily be wiped clean with a wet cloth.

Insects such as mealworms and maggots are held with the tips of the beak and the body juices are sucked out, the tongue tip playing an important role in this. Larger insects may be held in the foot and torn apart. The chitinous shell is not

# *Understanding Lories and Lorikeets*

eaten but discarded in the same way as uneaten pieces of fruit.

The tongue also has an important function in drinking. The head is held down at an angle and the beak is opened wide (so wide, in fact, that the upper mandible rarely touches the water surface!) and the tongue tip is placed in the water. The tongue papillae take up water, which is withdrawn into the mouth, and the process is continued until the thirst is quenched. Being tree-dwelling or arboreal birds, lories and lorikeets only occasionally descend to ground level to feed or drink. As far as drinking goes, they much prefer to lick dew or raindrops from foliage with their brush-tongue than descend to a body of water. The birds may perform some stunning acrobatics in their endeavors to reach water droplets.

## Sleeping

Breeding pairs with eggs or young normally will sleep together in the nest; nonbreeding birds have special "dormitory trees" where they congregate at night, much in the manner of northern starlings. Such communal roosts are often quite close to the nesting hollows of the breeding birds.

The nightly congregations are hardly peaceful affairs and there is much noisy squabbling among the birds as they vie for the best roosting spots, sometimes late into the night. On brighter nights, restless birds frequently will change trees in the quest for a more comfortable sleeping spot and renewed squabbles constantly will be breaking out. I often have observed communal roosts in the mangroves of lagoons and coastal islands, but sometimes also in orchards, parks, and gardens. They show little fear of man and I have seen them nesting and roosting in trees in busy town parks! Eventually the birds will settle for the night, only to awake at the crack of dawn full of renewed enthusiasm for feeding and breeding.

## Nomadic Behavior

Australian lories and lorikeets have a relatively nomadic life-style. This is due mainly to climatic factors, especially in the north where there is a long, dry season in which the vegetation becomes fairly dormant. There are thus few food sources for relatively long periods and the birds must forage over vast areas if they are to survive.

18

# *Housing*

Lories and lorikeets are exceedingly keen acrobats and will spend a great deal of their time clambering about on the cage or aviary wire, even on the roof where they will hang with their beaks and claws. A number of thick, natural perches should be provided in various parts of the aviary, but make sure that adequate flight paths are left. The correct position of perches is perhaps more important than the dimensions of the aviary.

In general, members of the genus *Lorius* are the climbers, whereas those in the genus *Trichoglossus* like to take to the wing occasionally as well as climb, so they should have larger aviaries. I have had good successes with indoor and outdoor aviaries with dimensions 5½ to 6

Many aviculturists use large cages with a deep tray to house newly imported birds. Like many parrots, lories and lorikeets prefer large aviaries.

feet (1.5–2 m) wide, 6 to 6½ feet (2–2.5 m) high and 6½ to 9½ feet (2.5–3.5 m) long. The night shelter is usually 5½ feet (1.5 m) and, if possible should be built higher than the flight, so that the birds will accept it more readily and sleep there (in a box) at night.

Provide a large, thick-walled nest box as sleeping quarters and place this as high up as possible, but leave some space above the top of the box and the wire ceiling as the birds usually love to perch there. Of course you can do this only in indoor aviaries; a garden aviary is too open to all kinds of dangers from above and a resting bird soon would become victim to a cat or bird of prey. One could, of course, use wide planks to protect parts of the roof.

The night shelter should have windows as large as possible so that maximum lighting is achieved. Windows should be screened with wire mesh to prevent birds from flying into the glass and injuring themselves. Wire frames also can be used to prevent escapes when the windows are opened for ventilation in the summer. Some thick, natural twigs also should be placed as perches in the night shelter. A feeding and watering station and a bath also should be located in the shelter. For obvious reasons, perches never should be placed directly over food or water containers.

Aviaries for lories and lorikeets should be preferably steel-framed and the mesh should be heavy gauge, as these colorful acrobats are excellent gnawers that can reduce a wood framed aviary to splinters in next to no time.

The foundations and the floor can be made of concrete. If you make a platform floor from mesh about 28 inches (70 cm) above the ground, it will make your cleaning chores much easier. Whether birds are kept in indoor or outdoor aviaries, daily cleaning is essential to remove droppings, food waste, and other debris that has fallen through the mesh floor. It is best to hose down with a strong jet of water from a hosepipe, so good drainage will be necessary.

# *Housing*

Great care should be taken in the siting of an outdoor aviary and, if possible, it always should be constructed so that the front faces south. If this is impracticable, then the next best choice is west. Always build with the best materials so that you won't have to make expensive renovations in just a few years' time. Remember, building materials keep going up in price, so you actually can save money by building for the future.

## Indoors

Many fanciers have a bird room containing a number of aviaries; cages are really unsuitable for these active birds. In such a special room it is quite easy to build a number of similar sized aviaries next to each other. The adjacent walls must, of course, be doubly meshed with the space between the wires at least 1½ inches (3.5 cm) so that the birds cannot attack each other's toes. I would recommend the use of wire mesh rather than solid walls as this is at least a little bit closer to nature in that wild lories and lorikeets usually operate in flocks and breed close together—so a breeding colony, as it were, is formed. It is best to place a single pair per aviary as captive flocks usually fight fiercely and severe injuries and fatalities are quite possible. Another advantage of mesh adjoining walls is that birds can learn more quickly to accept new foodstuffs (fruits, for example). Newly acquired birds will see other birds feeding on certain foods and copy them. With these intelligent birds it is definitely a case of "see eating— then eat!" Personally I have come across many cases of lories and lorikeets that have received nothing other than sunflower seeds and boiled rice to eat during transport. Such "foods" are far from ideal and you must get them onto a proper diet as soon as possible. However if these birds are in cages, out of sight of other birds, they will not eagerly accept the new diet offered to them. If however, they can see what other birds are eating, they will accept their new proper diet before the day is out. The only real disadvantage of mesh adjoining walls is that birds tend to be much noisier when they can see each other.

The walls of the bird room are best lined with washable materials, ceramic tiles being the most hygienic. There must therefore be sufficient room between the walls and the aviary walls. Good drainage is absolutely essential; I always strew a layer of cat litter under the aviaries. As already stated, build aviaries with steel frames and heavy gauge mesh—wood is soon destroyed by the birds. Place the nest box—which is also almost always used as a "bedroom"—in one of the corners of the front part of the aviary in order to facilitate inspection: all you need to do is have a little opening in the mesh and a sliding panel in one of the sides of the nest box. The false floor of the aviary, as already stated, is made of mesh and about 28 inches (70 cm) high; this makes cleaning beneath the aviary much easier. In fact, there are a number of aviaries built on legs!

Indoor flights should be easy to clean. Protect walls and floors with sturdy plastic sheeting. The wire netting and frames should be washed down at least twice a week with soapy warm water and disinfectant.

# *Housing*

I always like to make sure that my birds get as much natural light as possible, so small windows should be replaced with larger ones. If this is impracticable, then see if it is possible to install skylights in the roof. As lories and lorikeets are appreciative of adequate light, every effort must be made to provide them with as much as possible! They love to bask in the sun and this of course is good for their health. But do not forget that these birds also must have access to shade, especially in very hot weather, and make sure you arrange your windows and skylights so that both sunlight and shade are always available. Of course, good ventilation is important during warm weather so that overheating of the room is avoided.

In reference to good drainage, if it is financially possible, a sprinkler-system (as used in greenhouses) is very useful, but otherwise a garden hose punctured with many small holes will suffice for a "fine mist spray." Apart from a daily mist spraying, the birds should have a full water dish (at room temperature) until about one hour before they go to roost so that they can take a bath at any time.

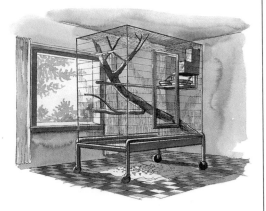

Lories and lorikeets are the most acrobatic of all hookbills and need a lot of room. Small and medium-sized species require an aviary that is at least 10 feet (3 m) long; the larger species, 16 feet (5 m) long.

Natural perches (see page 34) should be of varying thicknesses. I use branches varying from 1¾ to 2 inches (3–5 cm) in diameter, preferably from willow, poplar, beech, apple, or pear trees. These perches should not be too smooth (do not remove the bark) and should be fixed firmly in place so that the birds can copulate without danger of falling off!

In spite of the fact that lories and lorikeets may be kept in indoor aviaries, they still will require supplementary heating during the colder months (but depending, of course, on where you live). In their natural habitats they never experience temperature below the freezing point! In my experience, lories and lorikeets kept in warmed aviaries during the winter are more likely to produce good breeding results (see also page 22).

## Outdoors

Outdoor aviaries with good ventilation and rainproof shelters are also ideal accommodations for lories and lorikeets; dimensions and building specifications are as described for indoor aviaries above. If you want a "natural" floor (in other words you don't want to bother with a suspended mesh floor) you can use concrete with adequate drainage facilities. Hygiene is just as important outside, which means cleaning the floor and perches daily—preferably with a jet of water from a hose.

During warm, dry periods the birds should be regularly mist-sprayed and always should have access to a shallow bathing vessel. I use heavy, rectangular metal dishes about 2 inches (5 cm) deep, 17¾ inches (45 cm) long and 11¾ inches (30 cm) wide. The birds slide their bellies around the dish and flap their wings in order to get their backs nice and wet. Always remove the bath about one hour before dusk, however, especially in cooler weather, as birds retiring with wet plumage are more susceptible to chills.

# *Housing*

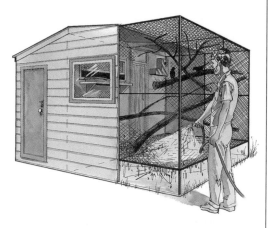

An outdoor aviary with enclosed shelter. Note the double floor and drainage.

In outdoor aviaries the birds are also only kept in single pairs. If you attempt to keep other species of parrotlike birds together with your pair of lories or lorikeets, you will have blood and warfare on your hands! Only nonaggressive, nonparrotlike birds can be kept with lorikeets but then, to be on the safe side, it is best just to stick with your single pair per aviary. The chattering lory (*Lorius g. garrulus*) and the yellow-backed lory (*L. g. flavopalliatus*) are both well-known warlike species and will not rest until they thoroughly have beaten up any other parrotlike birds with them in the aviary. This also applies through adjoining aviary mesh (see page 20) so you must continually be on the lookout for damage to the aviaries where birds could possibly get at their neighbors (and they keep trying, believe me!), with disastrous results—especially if you are not home at the time. Daily inspections are therefore essential.

All the aviary mesh (I use 1-inch square [2.5 cm$^2$), framework, and even the concrete floor of aviaries without a false mesh floor should be painted matte black with a roller and with latex or other lead-free paint. New mesh is reflective (and stays reflective for a long time), irritating the eyes

of people as well as the birds. It also makes it difficult to get a good view into the aviary. You will be surprised at what difference the black paint will make.

It is a good idea to make a small hatch with a sliding door in (preferably) the front of the aviary, opening onto a feeding platform. This will save you time when you feed and water your birds and will also give them minimal disturbance, which is especially important during the breeding season.

## Lighting and Heating

For indoor aviaries you can use a few 7-watt lamps so that the birds do not sit completely in the dark at night. Should they receive a fright, they will not then panic and fly blindly about (possibly resulting in a broken leg, wing, or even neck). Lighting is not necessary in the night shelter of an outdoor aviary as long as it has adequate large windows. At night outdoors it is rarely completely dark! Dimmers can be very useful in conjunction with artificial lighting and you will see your birds disappear into their sleeping boxes as soon as it gets dark in the aviary. Heating requirements will depend on where you live, but electrical supplementary heating of some sort is desirable where temperatures are likely to drop below

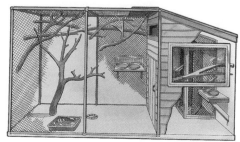

An excellent outdoor aviary. Note the concrete floor with drainage, and the sturdy perches set in the floor and hung across the aviary. The night shelter has a safety porch.

# *Housing*

41°F (5°C) at night. I use tubular heaters that are easy to install and are not particularly expensive.

## Nest Boxes

Experience has shown that L-shaped nest boxes are most eagerly accepted. Lories and lorikeets, especially when alarmed, have the habit of falling into the nest box on top of their eggs in their haste to hide. With a normal vertical box, of course, sooner or later eggs will be broken due to this behavior. Moreover, in a vertical nest box, the birds frequently gnaw at the entrance hole, making it lighter *inside* the box.

My experiences with L-shaped boxes have shown that it stays much darker inside and the incubating bird has a greater feeling of safety. Moreover I have noticed time and again that birds with L-shaped nest boxes almost always lay their eggs in the darkest (and thus safest!) part of the box — another reason for banning vertical nest boxes from the aviaries.

From observing lories and lorikeets in their natural habitats, I have come to the conclusion that these birds prefer to nest in horizontal rather than vertical hollow limbs, so that they can walk in to their eggs and young. This type of behavior is quite different to that of most other psittacines that like to select deep, vertical nests, into and out of which they must climb.

A further word about the regular vertical nest boxes that many fanciers still use. Before I started using the L-shaped metal boxes, I used vertical and horizontal wooden nest boxes. The nest box that I used for all *Lorius* species was always affixed among a bunch of strong twigs so that it was barely visible. The box I used was 13¾ inches (35 cm) square and 9¾ inches (25 cm) high, with a 3⅛ inch (8 cm) diameter entrance hole in the upper right-hand corner. Inside the box I placed a 2-inch (5-cm) layer of damp sawdust and pine bedding mixed together (50/50). The mating drive of *Lorius* species was, in my experience, at its height during March. The cock and hen kept each other in constant company, perching together, eating together, and behaving generally like a human courting couple. It makes quite an entertaining sight.

Nest materials (see page 32) are hardly utilized and you should refrain from inspecting the nest during the early stages as there is a danger you may upset the birds and keep them from breeding. When the hen spends all day in the nest box, you will know that she has begun to incubate her eggs.

During the breeding season, the cock gets much more aggressive than usual. This is a natural phenomenon that you must accept. Only the hen incubates the eggs; she sits very "tightly" and is fed by the cock in the nest box.

If all goes well, it is possible that a further brood will be reared so that at the end of the breeding season you should have four to eight youngsters "in stock." These can stay together in an aviary for some time.

During rearing of the young, the feeding schedule is the same as that for adult birds. Bear in mind that *honey must never be absent from the diet of lories and lorikeets.*

*Eos* species breed well in aviaries but also have been bred in a cage 67 inches (1.7 m) wide, 58 inches (1.5 m) high, and 37 inches (9 cm) deep (as a pair of red lories [*Eos bornea*] were bred in the Paignton Zoo, in England). The nest box was 15¾ inches (40 cm) high, 9¾ inches (25 cm) wide, and 6 inches (15 cm) deep, with a 4⅓ inch (11 cm) diameter entrance hole in the upper left-hand corner. Both eggs hatched and the young reared without problems — so you see that things don't always go quite by the rule!

Smaller species, especially those of the genus *Trichoglossus*, use their nest box as a bedroom as well as a nursery. Dimensions of 7 by 7 inches (18 x 18 cm) and a height of 11¾ inches (30 cm) are ideal — with an entrance hole 3⅛ inches (8 cm) in diameter. In the hollowed-out bottom of the nest box you should place a mixture of moistened forest moss and pine bedding.

These species also get the same menu during the breeding season as the adults get outside the breeding season (see page 25). The cleaning of the sleeping/nest box must be done very carefully as your "interference" may not be taken kindly by the birds. Outside the breeding season the boxes must be cleaned regularly as most birds use them as permanent sleeping quarters and they soon get filthy with the loose droppings of the birds. It is therefore best to make nest boxes with easily removable floors. Disinfect the floor well

and place a new layer of nesting material on top of a fresh layer of corncob litter. Make sure the inner walls of the box are also clean. A scraper can be used to remove hard-caked material and the walls can then be wiped with a wet cloth. Boxes should be cleaned regularly before accumulations of droppings become too great; the cleaning process only takes a few minutes. I personally clean nest boxes in the mornings, before the birds have their midday "siesta," or go to sleep at night. It is amazing how quickly the birds will get accustomed to your routine cleaning sessions.

# *Feeding*

I believe lories and lorikeets would be much more popular in aviculture if their feeding was simpler. A seed and fruit menu is by no means adequate to keep these colorful birds alive and well. Aviculturists must supply them with much more if they are to have success.

## Lory Diets

Some manufacturers fortunately have come up with some excellent lory diets and I have obtained the best results with:

• Lories Delight Dry Diet (ask for a free sample) c/o John Vanderhoof, P.O. Box 575, Woodlake, California 93286. Tel. (209) 564-3610.
• Avico Lory and Softbill Diets: Lory Life and Lory Life Nectar, c/o Cuttlebone Plus, 644 S. Isis Avenue, Inglewood, California 90301. Tel. (213) 776-6486.
• CéDé Lori/Handfeeding (excellent food for lories and lorikeets. Just mix with water for a complete and balanced diet. Also excellent for hand-feeding all types of baby birds.) Sunshine Bird Supplies. Inc., 8535 N.W. 56th Street, Miami, Florida 33166. Tel. (305) 593-2666.
• Roudybush Nectar Diets: Roudybush, P.O. Box 331, Davis, California 95617-0331. Tel. (916) 661-1726.
• Nekton Lory c/o Nekton USA, 14405 - 60th Street N., Clearwater, Florida 34620, Tel. (813) 530-3500. (If you own just one or two lories, you may want to purchase small quantities of this excellent but rather expensive product.)

It already has been ascertained that lories and lorikeets feed on a range of soft foods and insects in the wild and cannot be kept on a diet of seeds in captivity, even temporarily. So called "weaning" from soft foods to a seed diet is, in my view, animal cruelty! In the wild, lories and lorikeets feed largely on the nectar and pollen of eucalyptus trees and coconut palms, plus insects

and soft, unripe seeds. They also take buds and fruits. In captivity you must therefore give your birds the sort of variety they would find in the wild. In addition to the commercially available foods described above, I like to feed my birds L/M's Canary, Finch and Softbill Plus in a separate container. It contains honey, various insects (dried musca larvae, fly pupae), and fruits (various berries and raisins) plus a rich variety of vitamins, minerals, and amino acids.

In addition to commercially prepared foods I offer my birds a self-made mixture that is made in two parts. The first consists of a fresh-fruit salad, which may contain pears, sweet apples, pineapples, strawberries, various berries, carrots, and cucumber, depending on what is available. I do not use banana or citrus fruits as I have noticed that these can cause digestive disturbances.

The second ingredient mixture consists of equal parts of a good commercial brand of baby rice cereal, a cereal mix for babies (Beech Nut mixed cereal, for example) CéDé and/or L/M Universal Plus, and L/M Canary, Finch and Softbill-Plus.

I make a half gallon of each mixture, then mix the two thoroughly together with a wooden spoon before placing it in a blender for about a half minute so that I end up with a creamy, mousse-like mixture. This is placed in a 1.5 gallon (5.7L) bucket and the following additional ingredients are stirred in with a wooden spoon:

• 8 teaspoons V8 (Campbell, Camden, New Jersey);
• 8 teaspoons glucose (obtainable in health food stores);
• 1 teaspoon crushed cuttlebone or eggshell
• ½ teaspoon kelp powder (also available in your health food store);
• 2 teaspoons of a good bird multivitamin/mineral preparation (liquid or powder form), and;
• 10 teaspoons of honey.

# *Feeding*

A blender might be very handy to make a lory's "mousse" of fruit, grains, and vegetables. Honey added to the mix provides a readily available energy source.

The whole mixture is again placed in the blender (in quantities of say one pint at a time) for about a half minute. If necessary, add warm water to gain a creamy consistency (something like that of yogurt). The bulk of the mixture can be placed in 1-pint or 1-quart plastic containers (depending on how many birds you have) and deep-frozen until required.

The mixture is given twice a day; at about 7:30 A.M. and again at about 2 P.M. On warm days the mixture will sour quickly, and will do the birds harm, although they will still eat it and even continue rearing their chicks with it. Therefore, I would strongly advise fanciers in the warmer states, such as Florida and south California, to feed the mixture to their birds at least twice a day and to place it in a shady spot, to *prevent* it from going sour.

Making the mixture may seem to be a boring and time-consuming task, but after you have done it a few times you will find it is not such a chore as you may have imagined! And don't forget you can

Lories and lorikeets are extremely curious and playful. Their feet and grip are strong. A sturdy earthenware feeding dish is essential.

make large amounts at a time and freeze convenient quantities.

Self-made food mixtures are not only more economical than just using commercial foods, they are also better for your birds. I have had good results with this mixture for many years, including during the breeding season.

Depending on the species, I give daily supplements of shelled and/or unshelled sunflower seeds, millet spray, fresh berries and other fruits (see page 25), unripe and/or germinating grass/weed seeds, and fresh willow and fruit tree twigs.

However, do not forget that various brush-tongued parrots do well on some of the before-mentioned commercial diets, as long as they also have access to fresh fruit and vegetables. I have three pairs of blue-streaked lories that have lived on a staple commercial food for seven years. Not

A pair of perfect lorikeets.

# Feeding

only do they remain in first class condition, they produce offspring every year! Thanks to studies by Brian Rich and Stan Sindel, two Australian aviculturists (or should I say loriculturists?), it is now known that simple sugars probably are absorbed directly through the walls of the crop. They further recommend that fanciers should offer their lories and lorikeets a dry commercial diet in addition to the liquid diet, so that the birds are not sentenced to a life of "sloppy" food. Such a mixture of diets also will ensure that the droppings are not so thin and messy, but more resemble those of their wild counterparts (I have been able to ascertain that the droppings of wild lories are not watery, but quite well formed). Both of these experts also agree that a protein level of 15 percent is adequate.

I personally have had much success with Lories Delight Dry Diet (see page 25), which was formulated by the two Australians. Like John Vanderhoof, I give many of my birds 70 percent of this dry food mixed with 15 percent nectar and 15 percent fresh fruit and green food. The results are very encouraging, even with regard to breeding. This manner of feeding is quite simple and as far as the amount of work goes, similar to feeding seedeating parrots and parakeets. The dry diet mentioned has a consistency of fine flour and thus bears a semblance to flower pollen. In fact the texture is so like that of pollen that the birds accept it without question.

"Some lory species," according to Vanderhoof, "such as the Stella, the fairies, and the Duivenbode, are a bit more reluctant to eat the dry diet than others. When switched to a dry diet, these birds may initially lose some weight. If the weather is really cold, I increase the amount of nectar in my birds' diet. Some birds could lose weight if they do not receive enough nectar. The dry formula alone does not contain enough carbohydrates for extremely cold conditions (this problem does not seem to occur in the summertime). Lories are so active that nectar goes right through their systems. They need more carbohydrates than seedeaters do."

On Vanderhoof's recommendations I also have used this dry diet in the hand rearing of baby lories and lorikeets; all I did was mix it with apple juice and water and raised the temperature to 105°F (40.6°C). The advantage of this method naturally was that as soon as the birds were ready for weaning, I just had to leave out the apple juice and the water and give them the dry diet.

As far as seed is concerned I would make the following comments: as already mentioned several times, most lories and lorikeets are anatomically unable to digest dry, hard seeds. However, the Musschenbroek's lorikeet (*Neopsittacus musschenbroekii*) from western New Guinea, and the Iris lorikeet (*Trichoglossus i. iris*) from western Timor are two examples of species with which, over many years, I had great success with seed: *exclusively* millet spray, canary grass seed, various millets, black (oil) sunflower seed, oat groats, rape seed, wheat, buckwheat, and some hemp (in the colder months if the birds still had access to outdoor aviaries). These seeds formed 25 percent of their daily diet. Additionally, they were given 25 percent sprouted seeds, 15 percent greens (dandelions, endives, chickweed, and cooked corn) and 35 percent mixed fruits. Various species (especially those in the genera *Eos* and *Trichoglossus*) are fond of sprouted seeds and millet spray. According to Silva, a pair of Tahiti blue lories (*Vini peruviana*) at Loro Parque receive daily the contents of a small can of cooked corn, which they devour avidly. Whatever the species it is always worth occasionally experimenting with

Top left: Iris lorikeet.
Top right: A pair of Mitchell's lorikeets.
Bottom left: Goldie's lorikeets.
Bottom right: Yellow-backed lory.

# *Feeding*

diets, especially if you know the kinds of foods particular species will try. It thus has become plain to me that most species of lory and lorikeet are quite crazy about half ripe corn on the cob. This can be kept well in the deep-freeze and thawed out as necessary at any time of the year.

## Feeding Containers

Food for lories and lorikeets is best given in small, heavy earthenware bowls, that they will be unable to tip over or play with; something they love to do if given the chance.

The waste of food is another factor. Much food is strewn out of the dish as the lories reach deep into the food with their brush tongues and, with a shake of the head, toss the food away from their beaks. An acquaintance of mine had the idea of offering the food in the type of canary bath that is fastened over the door of the cage. Most of the food thrown about would then hit the walls or roof of the bath and fall back into the base rather than fly all over the room or aviary!

One disadvantage of such containers is that they usually are constructed of light plastic and the birds thus can drag them all over the place. They are also difficult to clean as the honey and glucose adheres to the surfaces. Whatever feeding vessels are used, they must be cleaned thoroughly every day.

It can be concluded that the fancier has various possibilities with regard to the feeding of his or her lories and lorikeets. These do not take up all of your free time, and the former "fear" of watery and messy droppings is no longer such a problem.

You can regularly vary the menu yourself by offering various "new" fruits including softened raisins, sweet apples and pears, currants, strawberries, apricots, fresh pineapples, blackberries, lemons, dates (without the pit), raspberries, rowan berries, peaches, plums, rose hips (most species love these!), hawthorn berries (remove the thorns from the twigs), wild elder, and figs. Remember that the avocado is poisonous as are the berries of the dwarf elder (*Sambucus ebulus*).

Finally, do not make the food mixture too thick as lories and lorikeets tend to push their beaks deep into the food and thick food would remain sticking to the beak. After a time, this can develop into an unpleasant crust, which could lead to secondary infections.

## Water

All captive birds must always have a supply of clean, fresh, drinking and bathing water. The myth that lories and lorikeets do not require water as they take in adequate fruit juices must be totally discounted. All lories and lorikeets drink (especially those receiving a dry diet)! Water should be checked several times a day and renewed if necessary. Colorful lories and lorikeets like to bathe several times a day, so bathwater must also always be available, even when the birds are nesting. In warm weather you can give the birds a shower with your garden sprinkler and most of them will enjoy this very much. Indoor birds also will appreciate a regular spraying with lukewarm water from a mist-spray.

# *Breeding Lories and Lorikeets*

Providing that lories and lorikeets are kept in optimum conditions and given a balanced diet, there is no reason why they should not breed. It should be the aim of serious aviculturists to make sure that the birds they keep reproduce in captivity. It is thus imperative that the birds are given all the requirements necessary to bring them into breeding condition. Fortunately, lories and lorikeets soon settle into a captive life and it is not unusual for totally unexpected clutches to be reared in the cages or aviaries of beginners who have little knowledge of the birds in question. I know of several cases in which lories or lorikeets have successfully raised a brood in a budgerigar nest box.

Every aviculturist experienced with lories and lorikeets will agree that these intelligent birds are extremely curious and therefore are more ready to quickly and regularly breed as long as you "stick to the rules." A few tips that follow will lead to the probability of good and regular breeding successes.

## A Good Pair

As most lories and lorikeets show little or no sexual dimorphism, it cannot be described as easy to make up a true pair, although there are various reliable medical methods that can be used (see below). Even if you have a true pair, it does not always follow that they will want to breed. Good pairs are formed with partners that are really interested in each other. If you have the opportunity to work with a number of birds of the same species (for example, if you cooperate together with other fanciers); then you can place couples of birds together and study the reactions; if there is no reaction or interest shown within a week, then give the *hen* a new male partner. Another method is to place birds singly in adjacent cages and see how they react to each other over a week to ten days. Believe me, there can be no doubt when the pair fancy each other! Place birds that have shown interest in each other together and see if they are in-

deed compatible. Pairs that are definitely cock and hen that have made no attempt to breed during the breeding season should be split up; new partners often lead to fast results! I have personally placed several birds of the same species together in a large aviary (with plenty of refuges or hiding places should the going get tough) in the hope that they would pair up. But even this was not easy; the birds remained tense and suspicious, making it difficult for any couple to pair up peacefully. Many lories and lorikeets cannot tolerate each other in captivity for long. Sometimes they will be peaceful for days on end, then suddenly there will be an outbreak of noisy, bloody warfare. I therefore recommend the two first methods to be safer and more effective.

If you have a nonbreeding "pair," you could possibly have two cocks or two hens or even two species! Many species and subspecies of lories and lorikeets are very similar to each other; the differences may be so small that even professional ornithologists find it difficult to determine one from the other. To make it even more difficult, couples of the same sex are not unknown to indulge in "breeding behavior." "Courtship" and "mating" and, in the case of two hens, clutches of eggs, are all possible. I once had what I thought were two cock birds for four years when suddenly I had eggs in the nest/sleep box. After endoscopic examination by a well-known avian veterinarian, I discovered that I had a true pair that, for some reason or other, had not shown any interest in breeding all the time they were together until that first clutch of eggs.

## Endoscopic Examination (Laporoscopy)

Under local anesthetic, a qualified veterinarian makes a small (few millimeters) incision in the left side of the bird's belly just below the ribs and inserts an optic fiber instrument. The left side is used because, in the hen, the one functional ovary is just left of center. With the instrument, which is known as a laporoscope, the veterinarian can look inside the bird. The instrument consists of a long, narrow, flexible tube with a system of small, narrow mirrors, and an optic fiber for light. It is thus possible to determine the sex of the bird; the male testicle looks cylindrical or elliptical, whereas the single functional ovary in an adult hen looks like a little cluster of grapes.

Relatively recently another method of sexing monomorphic bird species has been developed. Zoogen Inc. (1105 Kennedy Place, Suite 4, Davis, California 95616) has, after years of research, isolated a recombinant DNA probe called pMg1, which is associated with the sex chromosomes of diverse groups of birds. A probe, in recombinant DNA technology, is a small segment of DNA made up of a specific sequence of a similar stretch of DNA in a target sample. By analyzing the DNA sequence revealed by using the pMG1 prober, the sex of the bird being tested can be accurately ascertained, according to Zoogen Inc. As the DNA of an individual bird is constant throughout its life, this technique is not dependent on age or reproductive cycle.

The blood sample collection process is quite simple; a thin needle is inserted in a blood vessel in the toe and a drop of blood is collected. That, as far as the bird is concerned, is all! No anesthetic is necessary and the whole process takes less than ten minutes. The test is less expensive than laporoscopy, and is a noninvasive procedure with no postoperative requirements. Further information may be obtained from your veterinarian or direct from Zoogen Inc. (European fanciers should contact: Vetgen Europe, P.O. Box 60, Winchester, Hampshire, SO23 9XN, England.)

## The Right Nest Box

Over the years, various kinds of nest boxes have been tried and tested but the "ideal" nest box is yet to be found, and (as discussed on page 23), it is sometimes difficult to assess just what lories and lorikeets really require. Some general rules can be suggested, and one of these—a very important one—is that if you acquire captive bred birds, then the type of nest box you use must be similar to the one in which the breeding pair itself was raised. If you do not think this is the right box for your purposes, try the following: give them a choice of the box type in which they were reared, and one that you think is best; let the birds make their own decision.

Whether you use nest boxes made from hollowed out natural tree limbs or from thick planks is immaterial as long as the dimensions are right; if the box is too small, the incubating bird may accidentally damage the eggs or injure the young. Growing youngsters soon need plenty of space and, if the box is too small, the weaker chicks may get crushed or suffocated as their siblings squabble for food. If boxes are too large, however, the youngsters feel less secure, and will clump together in the darkest corner of the box. It is also important to make sure that the diameter of the entrance hole is not too big; the birds like the inside of the box to be as dark as possible; this is the reason why I have provided entrance hole diameters for most of the species described in this book, based on many years of experience of breeding these birds. It is always better to have the nest box entrance hole too small, rather than too large; in the former case, the birds themselves will soon enlarge it to their favored size. Sometimes they will even make the hole too large; in such a case you will have to repair it with a piece of strong plywood, in which you have made an entrance hole of the correct size.

It is a well-known fact that with few exceptions (monk parakeets and lovebirds, for example) parrotlike birds are not great nest builders. In the wild, most lories and lorikeets will work continually (while incubating or brooding, or when both birds spend the night therein) on the interior of their nest hollow with their powerful beaks. The wood dust and splinters will fall mostly into the

# Breeding Lories and Lorikeets

base of the nest hollow and eventually form a thick, soft layer. When the young hatch from the eggs they will thus sit on a comfortable layer, which also absorbs the fluid from their watery droppings, helping to keep them clean and dry. In captivity, the birds also will attempt to gnaw the inside walls of their nest box as they follow their natural instincts. It is recommended that you place a layer of damp wood pulp, mixed with washed aquarium sand, and pine bedding (or aspen bedding) in a ratio of 3:2:3. The birds will, however, frequently toss a great deal of this bedding out of the nest and make do with the gnawed wood debris. If you use a metal nest box (as discussed on page 23), then, naturally, you will have to supply a good layer of the aforementioned nesting material.

Wooden nest boxes must really be made of *thick* planks so that the birds cannot gnaw right through them too quickly, though in time they will manage to destroy all wooden nest boxes. Remember also that it is necessary for each nest box to be inspected and cleaned easily when necessary. It is thus best to have a little inspection hatch with a sliding or hinged door on the side of the box — large enough for you to insert your hand and check eggs or young. Personally, I like to include a fine mesh false floor about 2 inches (5 cm) above the bottom of the nest box and place the nest material on this. In the bottom of the nest box I drill a number of ½ inch (1 cm) holes for drainage (and with the watery droppings of lories this is certainly no luxury, believe me!). Metal nest boxes (see page 23) are also provided with a false floor (mesh stretched on a metal frame); I tell the manufacturers that I require this false floor, together with a number of round holes in the bottom of the box for drainage. These boxes are also provided with inspection doors and a removable floor.

The boxes should be installed as high up as possible, but not so high as to make it too difficult to comfortably inspect or clean them. I like to affix my nest boxes in such a way that it is possi-

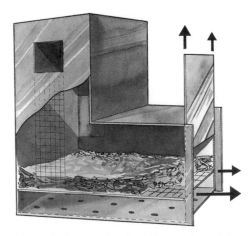

A lory or lorikeet nest box should have a wire mesh bottom to avoid an accumulation of the bird's watery droppings. The real bottom can be covered with pieces of charcoal, cat litter, and twigs to catch the droppings.

ble to inspect them without entering the aviary. A small hatch can be made in the aviary wire close enough to reach the control hatch of the nest box. With such a system the breeding birds are minimally disturbed, as the inspection can take place almost before the birds realize what's happening. I don't need to enter the aviary and moreover, as my birds are all quite affectionate, I will avoid the danger of leaving the aviary with birds hanging on my trouser legs! Experience has shown that my methods do not alarm the birds in any way. However, if the aviary is entered for nest inspection, it is a totally different matter. Your once hand-tame friends may become raging little furies that will attack immediately, using their sharp claws as much as their powerful beaks. As mentioned earlier (page 15), lories and lorikeets will defend themselves with their claws. When they are threatened (and a nest inspection may be regarded by the birds as a threat), they will quickly turn on their backs so they can keep the offender at bay with their sharp claws (their toes are extremely powerful). Then they may use their powerful

# Breeding Lories and Lorikeets

beaks, which (believe me) can cause serious wounds. A similar defensive attitude is taken by the birds if one comes too close to their youngsters. The parents will grip you with their claws and try to bite you with their beaks wherever they can—this is not an agreeable experience!

You should not, however, panic if your birds take this aggressive attitude; it is indeed their natural instinct and this must be respected. Doesn't every parent want to protect its offspring when danger threatens?

## Perches and Twigs

Lories and lorikeets are acrobats of the highest order, and an abundant supply of strategically placed perches is of utmost importance. Although a variety of perch thicknesses is essential for healthy feet, natural twigs are not always good for mating purposes due to their flexibility of movement. Although I have seen birds copulating on the ground, and I am also convinced that they will pair *in* the nest box, most pairings take place on stable perches. It is therefore important to have a number of thick, well-anchored perches in addition to other twigs and branches placed for exercise.

It is often best to place the hen in a new aviary first, the cock with her a week later. This allows the hen to get accustomed to the interior of the aviary and its furnishings, especially perches, feeding and drinking stations, and nesting and sleeping boxes. If she is a timid, quiet bird, it will give her a chance to "find her feet" before the more aggressive, male partner is introduced. In case of excessive aggression, the hen will already be "at home" and will know where to take refuge. Cocks that have been isolated for six months or so should never be introduced "cold turkey" but should be placed in a roomy cage that is placed in the aviary. If you have several aviaries adjacent to each other, you can first introduce

cock and hen through (double) aviary wire. In this manner the birds will get to know each other safely. However, a close eye must be kept on the pair for at least the first couple of weeks. Bunches of hay, willow twigs with leaves, and other twigs (from fruit trees, for example) should be placed around the nest/sleep box, in order to give the bird a feeling of security. You also can stick leafy twigs among the aviary wire for added seclusion, and as an insurance against the newly introduced birds flying into the wire and injuring themselves. For similar reasons, it is a good idea to do the same thing as the young are about to leave the nest. Twigs placed in the wires of adjacent aviaries will help cool the tempers of aggressive neighbors.

Before the breeding pair is introduced to the breeding aviary, both birds should be thoroughly examined. If necessary, clip the nails to the required length. Such tasks should not be carried out just at the *start* of the breeding season. It is important that you and your birds are friends that can trust each other well before there are eggs and young in the nest. Good breeding results are unlikely if you start messing around with the birds while they are breeding—the most important part of their lives! Only in a peaceful environment, with birds that fully trust you, are you likely to get outstandingly good breeding results. Always approach your aviaries quietly and behave in a gentle manner. Whistling and talking softly to the birds will help reassure them as you approach and it won't be long before they are coming, dancing, and bobbing, to greet you; they may even land on your trouser leg or jacket, or sit on your head or shoulder. Always offer the birds tidbits when you approach or enter the aviary (mealworms, germinating sunflower seeds, pieces of fruit), in order to develop the bonding between you and them.

It should be obvious that the offering of fresh twigs before and during the breeding period will help stimulate the reproductive drive. Wild birds go to nest as the trees come into blossom. The twigs you offer, with leaves, buds, flowers, and

# Breeding Lories and Lorikeets

even insects will awake the breeding lust in your lories or lorikeets. It is essential that lories or lorikeets kept in indoor aviaries (preferably with a good, broad spectrum lighting such as Vita Light) have a good supply of fresh twigs, just as those outside, for the entire breeding season. Did you know that the willow bark has a similar effect on birds as aspirin has on people? It therefore will do no harm to give your birds willow twigs all year-round.

## Temperature

As mentioned, it is important that lories and lorikeets kept in indoor aviaries should have a good artificial light source. The birds also should have about 12 to 13 hours of restful darkness, so the light must be switched off at night, preferably automatically by timer. However, indoor aviaries should not be kept in total darkness at night; a few 7- to 10-watt bulbs of the type used as childrens' night lights can be used, so that in case of disturbance the birds do not panic and fly into solid surfaces, possibly injuring themselves badly.

Experience has shown that the larger lories, such as members of the genus *Lorius*, produce the best breeding results at a temperature around 73°F (23°C), so the temperature should be maintained not less than 59°F (15°C) and not more than 79°F (26°C). The smaller species prefer a slightly higher temperature; my birds are kept at 75°F (24°C), but never higher than 79°F (26°C) or lower than 64°F (18°C). In connection with these temperatures, newly imported birds, once established in the aviary, generally go quickly through the molt and if they receive good care and diet they are likely to make serious attempts to breed during winter months. This is because the time agrees with the birds' natural cycle in the wild (winter here is summer in the southern tropics!). With the correct temperature, there is a good chance that the birds will breed in their first or second year of captivity. And if the conditions are suitable in indoor aviaries, there is no reason why they shouldn't breed during winter. You will, of course, have to keep an eye on these birds. As they are not exactly "veterans" of captivity, you must make sure that they keep their young warm and feed them adequately, especially if they start breeding during winter in outdoor aviaries. The crucial period falls between the seventeenth and twentieth days, when the hen starts taking more time away from the nest. The danger is that the young get too cold, lose their appetites, and perish. If possible, it is best to allow winter breeding only in indoor aviaries.

## The Clutch

Lories and lorikeets generally lay two eggs per clutch, occasionally three or more. The eggs are almost spherical in form and always plain white in color. Only the hen incubates the eggs; when the cock enters the nest box, usually towards evening in order to spend the night there, he will settle close to his partner but probably does not incubate as such. However, I have observed cocks that have sat upon the clutch for a short time when the hen has left the nest temporarily to relieve herself, though examinations of many breeding cocks have never revealed obvious brooding patches on their body.

While the hen incubates she continually emits "begging" noises, which are very similar to those emitted by the young (I have ascertained that the young develop the hen's call, a phenomenon that occurs in many, but not all birds) and which keep the cock busy bringing her food. When not feeding the hen, the cock sits close to the nest and keeps a close watch on the surroundings—something that often has been observed also with wild birds.

# *Breeding Lories and Lorikeets*

## Incubation Time

The average egg incubation time for lories and lorikeets is 22 to 31 days; smaller species having a shorter time than the larger. There is, however, an exception: the purple-crowned lorikeet (*Glossopsitta porphyrocephala*) from western and southern Australia and Kangaroo Island, has an incubation time of only 17 to 18 days!

In addition to a suitable temperature (see page 35), successful incubation requires a reasonable humidity. Experiments have shown that the ideal relative humidity for most species is 50 to 60 percent. A dry environment will cause eggs to lose moisture, the membranes harden and the young are unable to hatch—that is if they can make it to the day when they're due to hatch! Make sure bathing water is always available and do not worry if the hen disappears into the nest box with soaking wet plumage. Even in the wild, hens often have been seen going to their nests with wet plumage. During excessively dry periods it will do no harm to spray the aviary and its contents regularly with water to imitate rainfall.

## The Young

In many species, hatchlings are quite naked, whereas in others the young are covered with a white down. Naked youngsters get their covering of down usually by the second day. In two to three weeks the first light-brown feathers will appear. In the first weeks the young, thanks to excellent care from their parents, grow very quickly and have an enormous appetite. They open their eyes between the tenth and fourteenth days and when they can see the parents as well as hear or feel (through vibrations) them coming into the nest box, they will beg all the more. This is also the best time to place leg bands on the young.

Up to the sixteenth and twentieth days, most of the work usually falls upon the hen; but after this period, she will spend progressively longer periods away from the nest box. At this time, you must make sure that the hen continues to feed the young and that the temperature is not too low. At 3 to 4 weeks old, the tail feathers begin to grow, shortly after, the wing feathers, then the feathers of the head and breast. At 6 to 14 weeks, the young leave the nest fully feathered. At this point, they are usually much like their parents in general appearance. However, the parents will continue to feed them for a further 1 to 3 weeks, although they already will be able to help themselves to pieces of fruit and lory food from the food dish. The parents can get aggressive toward their young about 3 to 4 weeks after they leave the nest, sometimes earlier. Now is the time to remove the young to their own aviary—preferably one similar to that in which they were born and reared. It sometimes occurs that the hen starts a new brood even before

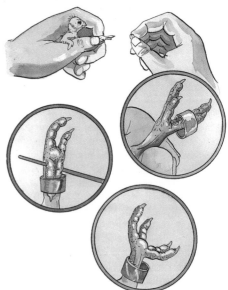

Banding a chick: preparing to slip the band (ring) on; the two front toes enclosed by the band; after you push the band down, the two back toes are pulled out with a toothpick; the band is in place.

the preceding brood has left, especially if she has had the choice of two identical nest boxes.

## Early Fledging

Occasionally, for one reason or another, certain young will leave the nest too early. If these birds are not adequately feathered and unable to feed themselves it will be necessary to hand-feed them. Use the same food that you offer to the parents. A plastic feeding utensil (available from your avicultural suppliers) can be used, or a teaspoon with the sides bent inward also can be used. Much time and patience will, of course, be required when you hand-rear lories or lorikeets. The following steps should be taken:

**1.** Warm, 100 to 108°F (38–40°C), bottled (not distilled) water or apple juice is added to the basic formula.

**2.** The mixture should be stirred, and more fluid added until it has the consistency of creamy milk; do not try to use a thick mixture that could congeal in the crop and cause digestion problems. If the problem should occur, it can be corrected by giving the bird some lukewarm water and gently massaging the crop. Any complications should immediately be referred to a veterinarian or more experienced breeder.

**3.** Use a syringe or medicine dropper or, preferably, a special feeding utensil or teaspoon that has had its edges bent upward. The temperature of the feeding utensil should be as close as possible to that of the mixture.

**4.** For purposes of hygiene, each baby bird should have its own dish and feeding utensil. Needless to say these all should be washed thoroughly and sterilized after each use.

**5.** Keep the formula warm during administration by placing the dish in a pan of water of the correct temperature, 100 to 108°F (38–40°C).

**6.** The baby bird is best placed on a hand-warm towel on a level surface.

**7.** Tap the bird gently on its beak with the feeding utensil to make it gape, if it hasn't done so already.

**8.** As soon as the baby starts swallowing and bobbing its head, deliver the mixture over its tongue with the feeding utensil.

**9.** You may steady the bird using a cupped (and warmed) hand during the feeding operation.

**10.** Rinse inside the bird's beak with a little lukewarm water, 100 to 108°F (38–40°C) after each feeding. Swab away any excess food from around the mouth and head, before cleaning around the vent.

**11.** Return the bird to its warm, 99.5°F (37.5°C) quarters (for example, a brooder or hospital cage heated and controlled by a thermostat); as the bird matures the temperature should be decreased very gradually until the ambient temperature is reached.

## Feeding Strategy

• *Hatching to one week:* The best time to take a baby bird from its parents (depending on the species) is between 10 and 21 days (generally

Spoon-, dropper-, or syringe-feeding is a task that should not be rushed! It is very important to mix fresh food for each feeding.

when the chick is just starting to feather but the later the better!). If hand feeding a hatchling becomes necessary, however, don't feed it for the first 10 to 15 hours, then start with one drop of lukewarm water; after one hour, another drop. Thereafter, it should be given a few drops of very thin formula every hour around the clock!

- *One to two weeks:* Gradually increase the consistency of the formula to that of creamy milk; feed every two to three hours. If warm, 90 to 95°F (32–35°C) and comfortable, the bird need not be fed between midnight and 5 A.M.
- *Two to three weeks:* Feed every three to four hours with creamy formula, from 5 A.M. to midnight.
- *Three to four weeks:* With a slightly thicker formula, feed every four hours. The birds can now be placed in a small cage with low perches and a shallow water dish, kept in a warm, draft-free spot.
- *Five to six weeks:* Feed creamy consistency formula three to four times a day, and introduce a free choice of sprouted seeds and lory formula to encourage the chick to feed itself.

- *Seven to eight weeks:* Give formula once a day. House the baby bird in a larger cage with feeding containers and a water dish.
- *Eight weeks on:* the bird should be off hand-feeding and taking a full adult lory/lorikeet diet.

## The Brooder

If you seriously intend to hand-rear baby lories or lorikeets, it will pay to have a brooder. An old aquarium or glass-fronted wooden box will make a good brooder. It can be heated from above with two 60-watt lamps (use blue or red colored bulbs to decrease light intensity) that are operated with a thermostatically controlled switch. Set the thermostat to 99.5°F (37.5°C) for the ideal starting brooding temperature. As the young grow, you may very gradually decrease the temperature, but do not reduce it below 86°F (30°C) until they are ready to be acclimatized to outdoor aviaries. As the birds grow, they will move in and out of the heat source, but this will do them no harm.

The best means of monitoring the chick's progress is to weigh it each morning before and after the first meal. The scale should read in 0.1 gram units.

# *If Your Lory Gets Sick*

Lories and lorikeets are generally robust and hardy birds and, if kept in roomy aviaries and given adequate care, should live long, healthy lives, breed regularly, and rarely become sick. In this country, thanks to the Association of Avian Veterinarians (AAV) (see page 90), there are now numerous veterinarians experienced in the treatment of sick birds.

Over-the-counter bird medications are not generally recommended as these sometimes can worsen the situation especially if the malady has been falsely diagnosed. It is thus a good idea to develop a good relationship with your local veterinarian; many are members of various bird societies and regularly attend bird seminars (the AAV has an excellent annual conference, attended by many national and international avian veterinarians and other scientists who present the results of their most recent research into avian medicine). The excellent *Journal of the Association of Avian Veterinarians* (see page 89) is a "must read" for everbody who takes aviculture seriously.

Now, although lories and lorikeets are naturally hardy birds, they do require certain specialized treatment, whereby *cleanliness* is of utmost importance. Not only must the food, water, and bathing vessels be thoroughly cleaned at least once a day, attention must also be given to the perches, which are soon made dirty by the birds continually wiping their sticky beaks on them. The rich lorikeet diet soon forms a thick coating on perches and provides an excellent breeding ground for possibly pathogenic organisms that could infect the birds, resulting in unpleasant consequences. Waste food such as fruit, bread, and seeds that may be thrown about by the birds must also be cleared away regularly before it attracts various, possibly disease carrying, vermin such as flies, cockroaches, mice, and rats. A regular inspection must thus be made of the feeding stations and their surroundings. Clean new cages thoroughly prior to use, to prevent zinc toxicity.

Breeding and sleeping boxes must also be regularly cleaned and disinfected. Hygiene is the keyword if you want to keep your lories and lorikeets in optimum condition. Fortunately most keepers of these birds realize the importance of roomy aviaries, usually with concrete floors and drains that allow daily hosing down with a strong jet of water. Earth floors to aviaries are not recommended, but if there is no alternative, the earth should be turned at regular intervals to keep it sweet and the top 6 inches (15 cm) or so should be renewed about once a year. Lories and lorikeets fortunately seldom go to the floor, so they are relatively less susceptible to worm infections than other kinds of parrotlike birds. Cleanliness of the aviary floor, though, will be an extra precaution against infection. Fecal samples ahould be regu-

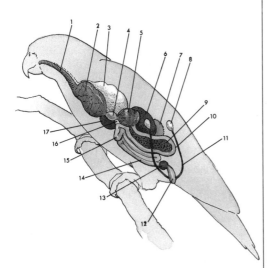

The internal organs of a lory:
1. Esophagus
2. Crop
3. Lung
4. Proventriculus
5. Gizzard
6. Liver
7. Spleen
8. Kidney
9. Pancreas
10. Duodenum
11. Ureter
12. Anus or vent
13. Cecum
14. Ileum
15. Jejunum
16. Gallbladder
17. Heart

# *If Your Lory Gets Sick*

larly examined at a veterinary laboratory for signs of infection.

## Mishaps

Aviary safety is of prime importance. Loose or unfastened wire, burrs on the wire, insecurely fastened perches or nest boxes, and so on all can pose risks of injury to these birds. Remember that lories and lorikeets are remarkably curious in their manner and will be continually inspecting every corner of their home. Electrical cables to which the birds can gain access with their powerful beaks will soon be gnawed upon—possibly with disastrous consequences! Keep an eye on the leg bands (rings) that the birds are wearing. Bands that are too large can easily get caught up on a snag, the bird may panic, and a fatal outcome is not to be ruled out.

Lories and lorikeets love toys. Look for safe toys made of untreated leather (rawhide), hardwood, hemp rope, and chain. Make sure that chain links are large enough to avoid accidents, such as catching the bird's toe. Watch for metal parts that might become loose. Don't buy toys that are hard to clean.

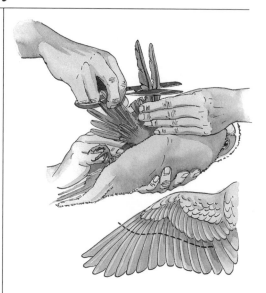

Wing clipping should be done with an assistant. Wear leather gloves and use a pair of sharp sissors. Always clip both wings. For "cosmetic" reasons, the two or three outer primaries are often left uncut.

There are also external dangers: rats, mice, weasels, cats, and owls are all animals that can cause untold damage to these birds if they get the chance, especially at nighttime. I have personally seen an owl catch hold of a lory that was resting on the aviary wire. The wire obviously prevented the owl from killing the lory immediately, but the bird received such serious wounds from the owl's talons that it had to be put out of its misery by the veterinarian. I now generally use double wiring on my aviaries and train all my birds to use the protected night shelter; I always place nest/sleep boxes in the shelter.

## Signs of Sickness

In addition to daily inspections of cages and aviaries for signs of external parasites, vermin, or anything unusual, it is necessary to keep a close eye on your birds. Good aviculturists will get to

# *If Your Lory Gets Sick*

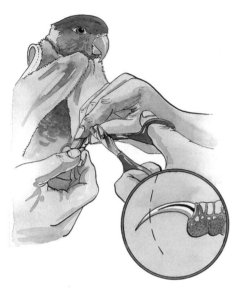

Nail clipping; be careful not to cut the part that is supplied with blood (the "quick"), but if it does start to bleed, a moistened stypic pencil should be applied. Note the proper restraining method. If you are inexperienced, work with an assistant and wear sturdy leather gloves. Better still, assign the job to your avian veterinarian.

know each of their birds very well indeed and will soon notice if a bird is behaving differently from normal. Apart from the natural seasonal changes in behavior connected with reproduction, molting, and so on, a sudden change in habit, however small, can indicate that a bird is falling sick. Excessive scratching, for example, may indicate parasites or skin infections. You can check by catching the bird and blowing its feathers aside.

Loss of weight (with the breastbone sticking out, for example) or obesity (increase in size) can indicate sickness and necessity for isolation. Wet nostrils, labored breathing, wheezing, or gasping all indicate some form of respiratory trouble. Examine the body for signs of wounds or tumors. Dull or inflamed eyes often may be a symptom of a disease. If the lower part of a hen's body is

swollen, it could indicate egg binding (see page 43), whereas a dirty, stained area around the vent would indicate an intestinal disease or digestive problem. All of these symptoms may be a forewarning of a more serious, possible fatal ailment, so it is important to be able to recognize the major diseases.

## First Measures

The first signs of sickness in lories and lorikeets are not always easily discernible, so that a careful daily inspection of your birds is essential. When a suspicious symptom is noticed, however small, it is better to take action immediately in order to "nip the problem in the bud" rather than leave it to chance. If you were over-cautious and the bird gets immediately better, you will have lost nothing but a little time, but it is always prudent to think on the lines of "better safe than sorry."

Sick birds are always best isolated anyway, just in case they infect their partners or other birds in adjoining cages. A respiratory infection, for example, can be spread easily through the air. All

An ideal hand postition for a lory to perch on. Use sturdy gloves for strange or large species.

41

# *If Your Lory Gets Sick*

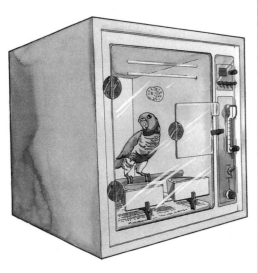

It is essential to transfer a sick bird to a hospital cage where you can maintain the temperature at about 86°F (30°C).

bird keepers are advised to invest in one or two "hospital cages." These are relatively small cages that are totally enclosed by solid walls except the front. A hospital cage should preferably have a double bottom with a grill so that droppings fall through to prevent possible recycling of infection. Hospital cages may be purchased from your avicultural supplier, or a handy person can quite easily make one. The cage may be heated with a suspended heat lamp, or you can rig up a system of varied temperatures using tungsten bulbs in the cage. If you use colored (blue or red) bulbs, the light will not irritate the bird but the warmth will still be available. The temperature for sick birds is best in the region of 85 to 90°F (29–32°C) and this can be maintained by moving the heat lamp up and down or using a thermostatically controlled switch. Whatever method you use, it is essential to have a thermometer inside the cage so you can keep an eye on the temperature.

Various ailments are quite often miraculously cured after a bird has spent a few hours under heat. Provide the bird with its favorite food and adequate fresh drinking water at all times. Even if it doesn't feed at first, the warmth will make it want to drink, which will be good for it, especially if it is feverish. As soon as the bird looks better you should not remove it right away, but reduce the temperature gradually by altering the thermostat or moving the heat lamp further away at intervals. Never move a bird straight out of heat into a cold aviary or it is likely to catch a severe chill.

All cages, aviaries, perches, furnishings, utensils, and so on must be thoroughly disinfected after any outbreak of sickness. Be careful in your own personal hygiene, use rubber gloves if necessary (and disinfect after each use), and keep clean—so as not to be the culprits who help spread disease among your lories and lorikeets! Of course, if a bird's symptoms get worse, or if they look very serious in the first place, then it is recommended that you contact your avian veterinarian immediately.

## Diseases and Injuries

### Aspergillosis

This is caused by the inhalation of particular fungal spores that grow in the lungs and air sacs and interfere with respiration. It is a potentially fatal disease that is very difficult to cure once it takes a hold, so prevention is the best course. The spores often lurk in things like moldy hay and corncob bedding, seeds, bread, chaff, straw, and so on. Always give only the best foodstuffs and keep your birds away from places where hay, straw, and so on are stored. Keep aviaries clean. A sick bird loses its appetite and rapidly deteriorates. It is best to refer such a disease to your avian veterinarian. Copper sulphate will kill the spores and a 1 percent solution should be sprayed on all aviary surfaces after an outbreak.

# *If Your Lory Gets Sick*

Restraining a lory. Always be gentle and never rest your hand on the animal's chest. Respect the beak, strong grip, and needle sharp nails. Wear gloves when handling strange or large species.

## Coccidiosis

Coccidia are microscopic protozoan parasites that rarely infect lories or lorikeets but cause serious coccidiosis if they do. The parasites are spread via the droppings and if the droppings of an infected bird (often a wild bird) contaminate your bird's food or water, then you may have a problem. Coccidiosis has a slow onset but late symptoms include rapid weight loss, diarrhea and bloody droppings, loss of appetite, and lethargy. Coccidiosis can be diagnosed from fecal tests and usually will respond well to sulfa drug treatment if caught early enough. Your veterinarian will be able to help.

## Colds

These can describe all manner of respiratory complaints caused by various microorganisms, allergies, or dietary deficiencies. Optimum care will vastly reduce all possibilities of respiratory infections but heavy breathing, wheezing, rasping, and gasping should be treated with urgency. Use a hospital cage (as in all cases of sickness) and consult your veterinarian who usually will be able to

diagnose the problem and recommend a suitable treatment.

## Intestinal Problems

As with colds, intestinal problems may be caused by all manner of things, but especially stale, spoiled, or moldy food. Additionally, many viral, bacterial, or protozoal infections, usually transmitted via the feces of other birds, can cause serious intestinal problems. The first signs of such problems are usually diarrhea—watery droppings that are often green, slimy, and foul smelling. The area around the vent becomes stained and dirty. The bird soon loses condition, mopes and fluffs out its feathers; it often will leave the perch and sit on the floor in some corner. Action must be taken immediately—move the bird to a hospital cage and refer to your veterinarian.

## Egg Binding

This is not a problem that is common among lories and lorikeets, but is one that can have serious consequences if not dealt with promptly. Egg binding is a condition in which a gravid hen is unable to lay an egg that is ready to come out. Substandard conditions in the breeding aviary, poor diet (hence, a deficiency in calcium, vitamins, and so on), breeding when too young, or starting too early in the season will all cause stress and can lead to egg binding, so you can already go a long way towards preventing it by carrying out only good husbandry. Despite all precautions, however, egg binding still occasionally will crop up in the odd unfortunate hen. During the breeding season, when it is known that birds are going to nest, you must keep a special eye on your hens and if a bird should look sick, sitting hunched up, usually on the floor and moving little, you can assume you have an egg binding problem. Pick up the sick bird and examine its lower abdomen where you will be able to feel the egg.

Another form of egg binding may be caused by a so-called "wind" egg—a soft-shelled egg

43

that arises as a result of a mineral deficiency in the diet. Mineral supplements, especially those containing calcium, should therefore be given at regular intervals.

If caught in time, egg binding is usually quite easy to cure. First use a plastic dropper to apply a few lubricatory drops of warm mineral oil or glycerine in the cloaca. Next, transfer the sick hen to a hospital cage with a temperature of about 90°F (32°C). The combination of warmth and lubrication usually will help the bird lay the egg. In circumstances where the bird has not laid after two to three hours of such treatment, a veterinarian should be consulted.

## Eye Diseases

Lories and lorikeets may be subject to a number of forms of eye infection, often resulting from complications of colds and secondary infections of bacteria or viruses. Other causes of eye problems may be a deficiency of vitamin A, or irritations caused by chemicals from aerosols, dust, and so on. If it can be discovered what is causing the irritation, you must of course remove the offending item(s) from the vicinity.

Bad hygiene, especially of perches, can help spread eye infections, so cleanliness is of utmost importance. Inflamed eyes are usually teary and often kept partly closed. The sick bird should preferably be moved to a quiet, warm spot (hospital cage) and its eyes rinsed with a 5 percent boric acid solution. Alternatively an antibiotic ophthalmic ointment may be applied, as prescribed by your veterinarian. Most infectious eye conditions respond well to such treatment and a complete cure can be expected within a few days.

## Feather Plucking

This condition does not often occur among lories and lorikeets but is not unknown. It usually starts as a result of boredom and often begins to-ward the end of a normal or abnormal molt; scratching and biting at the irritations caused by the growing feather can end up with the feathers being pulled out wholesale or nipped off at the base. Some parrotlike birds and especially cockatoos may even strip themselves naked!

It is not easy to cure a compulsive feather plucker (it is often solitary birds that start it—so try to make sure that all your birds are mated up) but first of all make sure that it has plenty to do. Provide it with lots of twigs from fruit or willow trees; hang up lengths of sisal string or rope for it to play with. Improve the diet and include regular vitamin/mineral supplements. If all else fails, it will be necessary to fit an Elizabethan collar to the offender. This can be made from stout cardboard and affixed around the neck so that the bird cannot reach its plumage with its beak but still can feed and drink. After a few weeks with such a collar and improved diet and conditions, the bird will probably lose its desire to pluck feathers.

Some birds develop a habit of plucking their young in the nest. In such cases it is not unusual to see the young leaving the nest totally bald on the head, neck, and part of the back. In serious cases the flight or tail feathers may even have been removed. In such cases, the young are often best transferred to foster parents or hand-reared.

## Fractures

If birds are always treated gently and protected from such things as naughty children with big sticks, boisterous dogs, or pouncing cats, fractures are extremely rare. If an accident should happen, however, it is best to consult an avian vet-

The male (front) of the purple-capped lory has a somewhat larger head than the hen.

# *If Your Lory Gets Sick*

erinarian, especially if you are a relatively novice bird keeper.

If a veterinarian is not available, and if you feel confident, you can treat a fractured wing or leg yourself. A broken, drooping wing is best bandaged with surgical gauze, after it is moved back into its natural position. Cut two slits in the gauze, then put both folded wings through the slits. Wrap the gauze around the back and cross it between the legs to prevent it from sliding off. The broken wing should be strapped along the body to make sure it heals cleanly. Make sure the bandage is tight, but not so tight as to asphyxiate the bird! Place the patient in a quiet, warm spot and provide adequate food and water. Use a cage without perches, preferably with a mesh false floor that must be cleaned daily. Some birds may have to be fitted with an Elizabethan collar to prevent them from pecking at the dressings.

In the case of a fractured leg, line up the severed sections and splint the fracture on either side with a couple of thin sticks (pieces of bamboo skewer are ideal). Keep the splints in place by winding gauze around the leg and binding it with surgical tape. Wind the gauze tightly as the idea is to restrict movement at the point of fracture. Another, more effective method, is to use strips of gauze dipped in a thin preparation of plaster of paris so that you form a mini plaster cast, but you may need practice under instructions from a more experienced person before you are confident in doing this by yourself. Remember that with valuable birds such as lories and lorikeets it is always better to use the services of a good avian veterinarian than to carry out "hit or miss" treatment yourself — you may not save any money in the long

run! It goes without saying that any injured bird should receive a thoroughly balanced diet with vitamin/mineral supplements.

## French Molt or Budgerigar Fledgling Disease

French molt is well-known to most bird fanciers but it is fortunately almost uncommon in lories and lorikeets. It normally starts in young birds while they are still in the nest. The cause of French molt is still not entirely understood, though there have been many theories and there is now evidence that a kind of polyomavirus could be the culprit. An infected bird will suddenly lose its newly acquired tail or flight feathers, sometimes other feathers as well. Of course, sufferers of this disease cannot fly and have to resort to clambering about with their feet. Some European fanciers affectionately refer to them as "infantrymen."

Unfortunately very little can be done about French molt. You may breed lorikeets for many years without seeing a sign of it, then, one day, it may suddenly appear among your fledglings without any apparent cause. Fortunately not all birds are affected. Some pairs may produce affected offspring in one brood and not in the next, others may never produce affected offspring, whereas others may produce affected offspring in every brood. In the latter case, it is best to give them a season's break from breeding and try your luck again in the following year.

## Frostbite

If you house your lories and lorikeets as I have suggested in this book, then frostbite should almost never be a problem. The most serious aspect of frostbite to aviary birds is damage to the toes, and in bad cases, the toes may be partially or even completely lost. Although unsightly, birds seem to get over such losses quite well. Frostbite can arise when birds get a scare on a frosty night,

Top: The Jobi lory from West Irian is one of the many subspecies of the black-capped lory.
Bottom: The popular chattering lory.

47

panic, and end up clinging to the inside of the open flight wire for several hours. To prevent this, you must make sure that the birds use their protected night shelters and, if possible, they should be locked inside for the night. There is little you can do for a case of frostbite of the toes except perhaps apply a little precautionary antibiotic ointment to the sore part.

## Mites

There are several kinds of mites that can affect birds. The red bird-mite *Dermanyssus gallinae* is perhaps the best known; it is a surface-dwelling mite that shelters during the day in crevices and cracks, in perches and nest boxes, emerging at night to torment the birds by feeding on their blood. The mites crawl into the plumage and get on the skin, which they pierce with their sucking mouthparts. A single mite does not do much damage, but in suitable conditions they can multiply to enormous numbers and cause untold damage, weakening your birds and spreading disease. Nesting birds can be constantly and severely tormented by these bloodsucking mites. It is therefore important that at each cleaning session you examine all parts of your aviaries, perches, and nest boxes for signs of mites.

Hygiene goes a long way toward preventing an infestation of these mites. Try to keep cracks and crevices to a minimum during aviary construction. Let the birds bathe frequently and try to keep wild birds away. Such measures also will help control feather mites, such as *Syringophilus bipectioratus*, that feed on feather and skin debris and can cause minor irritation, and the more sinister *Dermoglyphus elongatus*, that actually burrows into the feather structure.

There are several miticidal preparations suitable for the eradication of both surface-dwelling and body-dwelling mites. Many of these contain pyrethrin, a natural substance harvested from a kind of chrysanthemum flower. Though harmless to birds and mammals, pyrethrin preparations will eradicate mites, ticks, lice, and fleas. Take a look at the kinds of preparations available at your pet store or avicultural suppliers and select one that is suitable for your needs.

## Molting Problems

The normal molt is a natural phenomenon that takes place usually once a year. It involves the gradual shedding of old feathers worn out by the effects of wind and weather (temperature, humidity, sunlight), flying, preening, nesting, the young creeping between them for warmth, and so on. The main part of the annual molt normally takes place just after the breeding season and the adult birds usually look as though they need it. Parrotlike birds, however, molt almost continuously with the high point coming after the breeding season when the young have become independent. The molt therefore can be seen as a part of the whole breeding cycle. Under normal, healthy conditions, old feathers are shed slowly and replaced simultaneously by new growing feathers so that the bird never loses its ability to fly. The molt should be a restful time for the bird, though, at the same time, it will require a good balanced diet to provide it with the necessary proteins and minerals for new feather formation.

The problems associated with molting are known as abnormal molts. A bird may lose too many feathers at once and they may be replaced too slowly. It may molt in the wrong season (this can be dangerous in colder periods). These abnormal molts often are caused by extreme environmental factors such as unusually high or low temperatures, sudden changes in the weather, shock, disease, or fear.

A sudden molt brought on at the wrong time by shock or fear is known as a shock molt. This can be avoided by making sure that your birds are not subjected to any rough, frightening, or unkind treatment. It is important that they are not disturbed at night, so steps must be taken to keep cats, owls, weasels, mice, and rats away from the birds.

To summarize, birds that are kept in optimum conditions, are not shocked or stressed, and receive a varied, balanced diet are likely to complete the main molt without mishap and will emerge as fine, sleek examples of their postbreeding, exhausted, former selves.

## Obesity

Obesity means "very fat" or "stout" and, under normal circumstances, is not considered healthy. Fat birds do not breed well and often have shorter lives than their slimmer counterparts; they also may have respiratory and molting problems. Your birds will become too fat if they do not get a suitable diet and if they do not get adequate exercise to burn off excess energy. It often takes a long time for a bird to get too fat, and at first the owner may not even notice what is happening. To avoid obesity, try to keep your birds' diet under control and make sure there are plenty of opportunities for them to get adequate exercise.

## Preen Gland Infection

The preen gland is situated at the base of the tail and produces oil that is used by the bird to preen its plumage. Occasionally an abscess will form if the preen gland orifice becomes blocked. In such cases, a marked swelling will be apparent and the bird will be in obvious pain. The bird may peck and scratch at the offending spot and even pluck out feathers in the area. Consult an avian veterinarian, who will incise the abscess, remove its contents, and treat with antibiotics.

## Psittacosis

Psittacosis is a parrot disease but is also a general avian disease common in many other bird species and is then usually known as ornithosis; it is caused by an obligate intracellular parasite, *Chlamydia psittaci*. This serious infection occurs particularly in dirty breeding operations and can be brought in by imported birds, especially those that have been smuggled.

The symptoms usually start like those of the common cold with a runny nose, wheezy breathing, sometimes diarrhea, and general malaise. In later stages, the bird develops cramps, lameness, and paralysis before eventual death. Caught in its early stages, the disease can be treated successfully using antibiotics (usually chlortetracycline), although it is always best referred to an avian veterinarian. As humans are also susceptible to psittacosis (ornithosis) it is a notifiable disease and must be reported to the appropriate health authorities. Strict quarantine regulations in most developed countries are now keeping the disease in reasonable control.

## Salmonellosis

There are literally hundreds of species of the *Salmonella* bacillus, many of which are pathogenic to birds. The rodlike bacteria can cause diarrhea, inflamed joints, and nervous disorders. The infective organisms are transmitted via the droppings or saliva (such as in parent birds feeding their young) of infected birds or mammals. Salmonellosis can occur in many species of birds and mammals (including humans) and can be transmitted freely from one creature to the next in unhygienic conditions.

The bacteria are usually ingested with infected food and enter the wall of the intestine. They interfere with the digestion and cause diarrhea that is often foul smelling, soupy, or green or brown colored. (A green color in the droppings also can indicate a gallbladder infection. Consult a veterinarian immediately!) At the later stage, the bacteria enter the bloodstream and infect all parts of the body. They are particularly troublesome in the bone joints where they cause swelling and intense pain. Eventually the internal organs, such as the liver, kidneys, and heart, also become infected. Once in the nervous system and brain, loss of balance, crippling, and paralysis can occur. With such a serious infectious disease, it is important that a veterinarian is consulted. Thorough disinfection and cleaning of all cages, aviaries, surroundings, and equipment is necessary after an outbreak.

## Scaly Face

This is caused by a burrowing mite (*Knemidocoptes pilae*), numbers of which attack the skin area around the beak and eyes and, in serious cases, also on the legs and toes. Though common in budgerigars, the condition is fortunately rare in lories and lorikeets but does occur occasionally. The little arachnoidal parasites burrow and reproduce just under the skin, causing inflammation and rough, scaly growths. Untreated, serious deformity of the beak can occur and the disease will spread among all your stock.

Treatment includes application of benzyl benzoate, petroleum jelly, mineral oil, or glycerine, to the crustlike formations. If using oily substances, be sure not to get any on the plumage; a cotton swab can be used to good effect. Burn any of the scabbing that comes away and continue treatment daily until complete cure is effected. Serious cases should be referred to a veterinarian who will be able to treat with more specialized drugs.

## Sour Crop

This is usually the result of blockage of the crop-exit, due to something the bird has eaten, a small feather, for instance. The contents of the crop begin to ferment, releasing carbon dioxide and resulting in the crop becoming bloated with gas. The sick bird will vomit a frothy liquid and its head and beak will become stained with mucus. Catch the bird, hold the head downward, and gently massage the crop to expel the gas and some of the accumulated fluid (which will be mainly water). Any complications should be referred to an avian veterinarian for advice.

## Worm Infections

It is difficult to avoid worm infections in birds that are kept in outdoor aviaries. Wild birds are continually releasing worms or their eggs via their droppings and some are bound to fall into aviaries at some stage. Regular cleaning and hosing of aviary floors and occasional disinfection with a solution of bleach or similar will go a long way to help avoid infestations.

Threadworms (*Capillaria*) are round, thread-like parasites that grow in the crop or intestine of the bird. The adult worms then lay eggs that are passed out with the droppings ready to spread to more birds. Loss of weight and diarrhea may be signs of infestation. There are several good proprietory vermicides that can be administered to your birds—ask your veterinarian for advice.

Roundworms (*Ascaris*) start as long larvae that develop into adult worms in the birds' intestines. The adult worms lay eggs that, like threadworm eggs, are passed out with the feces; symptoms of infestation include loss of weight and diarrhea. Most worm infestations can be diagnosed by examination, in a veterinary laboratory, of fecal samples from the birds.

## First Aid Equipment

It is strongly recommended that serious aviculturists maintain a basic set of first aid equipment and medicines so that they are always prepared in case of an emergency. The following is a list of suggested basic requirements:

**Infrared lamp:** (60- to 100-watt bulb) for emergency application of warmth.

**Hospital cage:** either purchased or homemade—try to have a look at a number of options before making your choice.

# If Your Lory Gets Sick

**Thermometer:** for monitoring temperature in the hospital cage—get a good one!

**Adhesive tape:** has multiple uses—use a half-inch roll.

**Sterile gauze pads**

**Cotton-tipped swabs**

**Sharp scissors or nail clippers**

**Feeding tubes:** use 8F or 10F tubes, which should be available from your veterinarian.

**Syringes or plastic medicine or eye droppers:** for administering oral medication.

It is generally not recommended that you keep a large stock of medicines and drugs, especially if you forget which is which, or if you do not know what a medicine is for. All medicines must be treated with respect and kept away from children and unauthorized adults (preferably in a locked first aid cabinet). Most medicines will be prescribed by your veterinarian for specific purposes and any leftovers should be discarded once the job has been done. However, the following is a list of basic medications that may be kept in stock and used for simple ailments:

**Kaopectate or Pepto-Bismol:** for diarrhea and regurgitation. Soothes and coats the digestive tract. Dosage: 2 or 3 drops in the mouth every four hours administered with a medicine dropper.

**Maalox or Digel:** for crop disorders. Soothes the inflammation and eliminates gas. Dosage: 2 or 3 drops every four hours.

**Gevral protein:** for loss of appetite. Always mix 1 part with 3 parts Mull Soy, which is also a good source of minerals and vitamins. Administer 2 to 3 ml of the mixture via a stomach tube, two or three times daily. Your veterinarian will show you how to do this.

**Karo Syrup:** for dehydration and as a provider of energy. Mix 4 drops to 1 quart (1 L) of water and administer 8 to 10 drops of this solution with a dropper every 20 to 30 minutes until there is a marked improvement, then gradually increase the periods between treatments until a complete recovery is effected.

**Styptic powder or stick:** to stop bleeding, but do not use on areas near the beak.

**Goodwinol, mineral oil, Scalex, Eurax, Vaseline:** for scaly face or scaly leg. Mineral oil also may be used as a treatment for constipation, crop impaction, or egg binding. Administer 2 drops into the mouth with a dropper twice a day for two days. Be very careful that the oil does not enter the lungs (it can cause pneumonia) or soil the plumage.

**Betadine, Domeboro solution, A&D ointment, Neosporin, Neopolycin, Mycitracin, Aquasol A:** for skin irritations. Domeboro is used as a wet dressing: dissolve 1 teaspoon or tablet in a pint of water. A&D is excellent for small areas. Neosporin, Neopolycin, and Mycitracin contain antibiotics. Aquasol A is a cream that contains vitamin A. Any of these remedies may be applied to the affected area twice daily. Note: Most of these products are petroleum based, hence, they never should be used on feathered areas!

**Lugol's iodine solution:** for enlarged thyroid (goiter). Half a teaspoon of Lugol with 1 ounce of water; place 1 drop of this mixture in 1 ounce of drinking water daily for two to three weeks.

# *Lories And Lorikeets*

## Genus *Eos* (Red Lories)

This genus of mainly bright red, slimly built birds, contains six species and about 12 widely recognized, and some disputed subspecies. The total lengths of the birds vary between 9 and 12 inches (23–30 cm). The fairly short, broad tail, and the strong, yellow-orange to orange-red beak are characteristic of the species. The upper mandible is strongly hook-shaped and sharp. Though largely red, the plumage is sometimes marked with black, sky-blue, or deep-purple patches; most youngsters possess darker or black spots on their juvenile primaries. In spite of the fact that these birds are in no way delicate, I consider it best to bring outdoor aviary birds indoors for the winter or provide them with a heated shelter, at least in the colder regions. In Florida or south

The violet-necked lories (*Eos s. squamata*) are very aggressive toward their own species and other large birds with a lot of red in their plumage!

California, however, I have seen *Eos* species doing well in outdoor aviaries (with a night shelter) all year-round.

In general, the members of this genus are adept and rapid fliers, although their wings are perhaps anatomically not quite so strong as those of the genus *Trichoglossus* (wedge-tailed lories). The voice of the red lory cannot be described as attractive; it is loud and piercing. Most species occur in fairly remote and difficult to reach, montane rainforest areas, where they live in pairs or small groups. It is therefore understandable but unfortunate that relatively little is known about their ecology. However, more is known about the habits of the species, which occur along the inhabited coastal strips. These are not only frequently kept as pets in their native lands, they are also regularly available on the pet market at reasonable prices; this in spite of their shrill, piercing voices and their musky odor (this is especially so, according to T. Pagel and R. Low, in the black-winged lory, *E. cyanogenia*), which does not make them popular with *every* aviculturist. Once acclimatized and used to their diet and housing, they usually will breed quite well, especially if the temperature can be maintained around 93°F (34°C). With their really stunning colors, their playful antics, and their willingness to quickly become tame, I am convinced they deserve a lot of attention!

In addition to the normal lory diet and a variety of soft fruits they will take quite a lot of live food, especially if they are rearing youngsters. For the first few days, hatchlings often are reared on mealworms, maggots, and similar food, in addition to the normal "crop milk." Grass and weed seeds both fresh and in germinated form are eagerly eaten, but the quantity eaten may vary from day to day. My *Eos* species would eagerly attack unripe corncobs, both in and out of the breeding season. I would recommend that all *Eos* species are kept in single pairs as they are very aggressive toward all other birds, especially other parrotlike birds.

# *Lories And Lorikeets*

## Red Lory—*Eos bornea bornea*

**Synonym:** Moluccan Lory

**Distribution:** Found in the Moluccan Islands of Amboina and Saparura.

**Description:** These beautiful and powerful birds, with their characteristic round heads, are rather variable in size. Ground color is light to tomato red, with black in the primaries. The speculum is red. The secondaries have black tips. A 0.8-inch (2-cm) wide blue band runs over the greater wing coverts. The undertail coverts are dark blue; the area around the vent is cobalt blue. The beak is orange-red to yellow (captive birds, especially, develop a conspicuously yellow beak in two to three years); the iris is orange-red, the naked eye-ring is gray-blue, and the feet are gray. Juveniles have a black beak and the plumage is duller with a gray-black sheen. They show a somewhat darker pattern but this can be very variable.

**Length:** 11.8 inches (30 cm); wings, 6.7 inches (17 cm); tail, 4.3 inches (11 cm).

**Habitat:** Generally found in wooded country, especially in mangrove forests. Sometimes in parks or near agricultural land but only in areas where there is adequate tree cover; they tend to

The red lory has bred in large cages! However, it is essential that this species is the sole occupant of the accommodation.

avoid open areas. They are especially at home in flowering *Eugenia* and *Erythrina* trees where they forage for nectar, pollen, and insects. They are also fond of ripe fruits and berries, and occasionally will partake of unripe (soft) seeds. The red lory is well known for its shrill voice, which it uses continuously. It is very adept on the wing, with a fast and straight flight path.

**Aviculture:** Unfortunately the voice, as mentioned above, is somewhat nerve splitting and is one of the few reasons not to keep red lories. You must, of course, consider your neighbors before you acquire such noisy birds, which are best kept in an outdoor aviary. Conversely, a healthy, full feathered example of this species is a feast for the eyes. A pair of these birds usually will breed in a roomy aviary, minimum 12 feet (4m) in length, indoors or preferably outdoors. The two eggs, 1.2 by 0.9 inches (30.2 x 24.2 mm), are incubated solely by the hen and hatch in about 26 days. As with all *Eos* species, the young start with a white down, which changes to gray in about eight days. The eyes are opened at two weeks and feathers appear all over the body within a month. The cock feeds the hen on the nest and both parents feed the young, which leave the nest in seven to nine weeks though are still looked after by the parents for about another month. During the breeding season, the normal diet must be supplemented with maggots, sweet apple, banana, grapes, soaked raisins, various berries, and shelled sunflower seeds. Some specimens will take unshelled sunflower seeds, which they not only take eagerly but shell adeptly! Fledglings also are very fond of sunflower seeds.

**Remarks:** Once independent, the young are best separated from the parents, which are likely to become aggressive, sometimes with disastrous results.

I have noticed that parents with chicks in the nest like to feed them with insects, especially maggots (this also applies to the birds in the wild), but also ants' eggs and fly pupae; more so than any lory species I have had or still have. At one week old, the young are fed with all kinds of soft fruit and berries by their parents. About 8 to 11 months after leaving the nest, the young are in full adult plumage. During this time, I give my birds canary grass seed, soaked oats, corn-on-the-cob, water-soaked, stale brown bread, and lory food (see page 25).

During the winter, the birds must be kept at a minimum of 50°F (10°C). Newly imported birds must be kept at a minimum temperature of 68°F (20°C). Once acclimatized, these are hardy birds that can be kept summer and winter in an outdoor aviary provided it has a dry, draft-free night shelter. It is best to place the nest box inside the shelter, high up in one of the corners, but so that the entrance hole is in some light. Enough space for a bird to sit on top of the nest box should be allowed. During really cold periods, it is best to shut the birds in the night shelter and make sure that the temperature does not fall below 50°F (10°C).

These birds are somewhat playful in their behavior and become very trustful toward their owner if he or she makes regular daily appearances. Do not forget to place playthings in the aviary, such as hemp rope, commercial toys, and similar items.

I once kept a pair that, due to circumstances beyond my control at the time, had to be housed in a canary breeding cage, which was 3⅓ feet (1 m) long by 21⅔ by 21⅔ inches (55 x 55 cm). This cage stood in the middle of the bird room surrounded by other cages all occupied by different species of birds. I spent a lot of time in this bird room and also received regular visits from many other fanciers; in short, this bird room was not exactly a haven of tranquility. Nonetheless, the pair of lories decided to breed. The nest box was 13¾ by 13¾ inches (35 x 35 cm) with a height of 17¾ inches (45 cm) and stood on the floor of the canary cage! The birds remained calm and friendly in spite of the pressure, and they were very trusting—accepting pieces of fruit and maggots from my daughter and even from total strang-

ers. As they knew me very well, I could scratch them on the head. It was sometimes embarrassing when the birds copulated before a small audience . . . you must understand that I was not expecting a successful breeding as I always had been led to believe that this species required a quiet, well-planted aviary. (I was rather surprised about the latter, considering the gnawing powers of these birds, which would totally destroy any plants in no time at all.) One day I noticed that the hen had a very plump abdomen and was spending more and more time in the nest box. A few days later I could no longer control my curiosity, so I peeked in the nest box; there lay the first white egg! A second egg never appeared, but four days after the first egg (and the period between eggs is usually one to three days) the hen began to incubate; the cock accompanied her at night in the nest box but probably did not take direct part in the incubation as this is not usual in lories. However they do keep the hen company at night and I have even observed this among wild lories of various species with or without eggs or young. The hen left the nest often during the day to feed and to bathe; I timed the periods she was off the nest and sometimes it was only 15 minutes, but it could be a half hour or even 45 minutes! I can honestly say that I did not have much hope of the egg hatching. You will therefore imagine my astonishment when, on the twenty-sixth day, a healthy, lively chick hatched from the egg. This was fed by the hen after about 20 hours and assisted by the cock three days later. Precisely three months later the pair were still in the canary breeding cage; the youngster had quickly grown up and was now housed in a large outdoor aviary. The pair decided to breed again and two eggs were laid but these were unfortunately infertile. Two months later however, a further two eggs were laid; these were fertile and after an incubation period of 25 days, the first youngster hatched; the second arrived two days later. For the first few days, the hatchlings were fed with the so-called crop milk and, on inspection, it was impossible to see if the youngsters

# Lories And Lorikeets

had food in their crops. At first I was worried that they were not being fed, but after a few days the situation improved; I gave them unripe grass and weed seeds, which soon could be seen through the walls of the youngsters' crops.

As they got older, the color of the crop contents changed so that I could see that the main food being given to the young was now the soft lory diet; also, quite a lot of millet spray seed was fed to them. When the youngsters were 14 days old, I ringed them with a 9/32 inch (7mm) leg band; I thought the 15/64 (6 mm) band was too small and I was proven correct when a colleague had great difficulties when he attempted to use this smaller size. Although the parents were quite aggressive when I removed the young to ring them, all was well when I returned them to the nest and they reaccepted them with no problems. As a precaution, I had rubbed my hands first in some of the debris from the nest so that the "human smell" was not transferred to the young, which could have upset the parents even more. With regular inspections, I could see that the young were born covered with white down that changed to gray in eight to ten days. At 21 days, the first feather shafts came through and the plumage was complete in 10½ weeks, apart from the wing and tail feathers, which still required a little more growth.

At three months of age, the young left the nest but were fed by the parents for at least three weeks; they were then removed from the cage as the cock started behaving aggressively toward them. The fledglings are quite similar in appearance to the adults. Only the red color was a little duller and there was more blue in the wings. At the same time, they had two blue bands on the sides of the thighs but these disappeared after the first molt, just like the black beak, which turned red when they were about seven months old. The youngsters were exceedingly tame and would land on my head or shoulder as soon as I entered the aviary, testing my face and especially my ears with their brush tongues. Over four years I was

fortunate in being able to raise 15 youngsters from that pair!

**Subspecies: The Buru Red Lory** (*E. b. cyanonothus*) from Buru, Indonesia is somewhat darker red in color, and the red wing coverts have a bluish-gray sheen. The rump of the young hen is frequently light blue; the primaries are almost black with a greenish sheen. The upper and undertail coverts are usually dull red with light, olive-green undertones. The feet are gray-black, the beak is beige-orange. Young cocks usually have blue ear patches, some blue feathers on the neck, and quite a lot of blue on the belly and rump; in any case more than the hens. Adult birds are much redder but both young and adults can be quite variable. **Length:** 11 inches (28 cm); wings, 6.2 inches (15.5 cm); tail, 4 inches (10 cm). These birds have a similar life-style to the nominate form but, as I have observed in the wild, are much quieter in and around the nesting sites. Captive specimens remain quite shy and have a habit of hiding behind thick branches, nest boxes, or in similar places when you enter the aviary. Regular breeding successes have been reported.

The **Bernstein's Red Lory** (*E. b. bernsteini*) occurs on the Kai Islands. This subspecies is very similar to the nominate race and differs perhaps only in size. **Length:** 12.6 inches (32 cm); wings, 7.1 inches (18 cm); tail, 5 inches (12.5 cm). This race may be more common in captivity than realized due to its similarity to the nominate type.

The **Rothschild's Red Lory** (*E. b. rothschildi*) from Ceram is also different to the nominate form only by size. **Length:** 10.6 inches (27 cm); wings, 6.2 inches (15.5 cm); tail, 4 inches (10.5 cm). To be sure of the subspecies in such cases, one must know exactly from where newly captured specimens came. In the wild, these birds are common along the coast but may also be seen in the hills to 4,000 feet (1250 m). They love to forage in the crowns of *Eugenia* trees, where they seek out the pollen and nectar from the flowers and take the occasional insect. I have had the opportunity of observing this subspecies in the wild.

# Lories And Lorikeets

One striking aspect of their behavior I observed was flocks of the flying birds circling around on moonlit nights and eventually swooping into palm trees where they presumably foraged for food. In captivity, these quite affectionate but shy birds are regularly bred. It is important to separate the youngsters from their parents as soon as they can look after themselves. I have discovered that this is one of the most aggressive *Eos* types with regard to attacking their independent young; I have seen cases whereby a cock bird in renewed breeding condition has harassed his previous brood to death.

## Blue-streaked Lory — *Eos reticulata*

**Synonym:** Blue-necked Lory

**Distribution:** Found in the Tenimbar Islands (Indonesia); the species also has been introduced to the Kai Islands and Damar Island.

**Description:** The base color is dark red. A blue-violet eye line begins under the eye and widens towards the neck in the shape of a fan. The blue is marked with lighter patches giving the impression of white stripes. The rump, belly, and

The blue-streaked lory was first bred in the United States in 1939. The nesting period may be as long as 12 weeks!

thighs are red. The red speculum is richly decorated with light centered, dark blue feathers. The wings are red with dark blue to black markings and black feather tips. The primaries are mainly black with reddish sheens. The upper side of the tail is brownish gray, the underside is matte red. The beak is orange-red, the iris is reddish-brown, the narrow, naked eye-ring is gray, and the feet are dark gray. With adequate comparison material it can be ascertained that the hen's beak is frequently somewhat slighter than that of the cock, but it is otherwise difficult to determine the sexes. Juveniles have black-blue edged, red breast feathers and a dark gray beak.

**Length:** 12.2 inches (31 cm); wings, 6.7 inches (17 cm); tail, 5.1 inches (13 cm).

**Habitat:** Unfortunately the wild habits of this lively species are poorly known, though it is generally common in its native haunts. In general, its habits are probably very similar to those of other *Eos* species.

**Aviculture:** This colorful species is undoubtedly one of the most beautiful members of the genus. It is an exceedingly lively bird that demands much attention. It generally becomes tame and affectionate once acclimatized and accustomed to its new surroundings. These birds require lightly heated, 50°F (10°C), winter accommodations. I find these to be rather comical birds that spend the day tumbling and playing; they are thus more suited to a roomy aviary than a cage. They like to hang from the aviary wire or from a perch; even when you enter the aviary. My birds have the habit of holding their heads low along the perch close to the food hopper and let out a not unattractive chirp as if to be asking what tasty morsels are next on the menu.

**Remarks:** The courtship behavior is also amusing to watch. They usually walk along the perch one foot over the other toward each other and, as they approach each other, they open up the wings like arms and appear to be cuddling and kissing. Mating then takes place; this can last for several minutes.

# *Lories And Lorikeets*

The first specimens were introduced to the public at the London Zoo in 1862. The first American breeding success was in California in 1939 and in 1972 (!), the first in England. During the 1970s this species became quite a regular import, especially in Europe. The two white eggs, about 1.1 by 0.9 inch (29 x 23 mm), are incubated by the hen alone and the young hatch after about 26 days. The young are a little slower in development than most other members of the genus. The first feathers appear after six weeks and they are fully feathered at 80 to 84 days. The young leave the nest at about 14 weeks and are fed by the parents for a further two weeks; the cock is especially busy in providing them with food. After these two weeks they become quickly aggressive towards the young, which should thus be moved to separate roomy quarters. At first the young in the nest are fed with various insects (I give them mealworms, maggots, and small ant pupae), later with standard lory food, plenty of fruit, and green food. Fresh green twigs also should be part of the menu. Colleague Pagel noted that newly imported birds are rather shy and would try to hide when approached—the cock sometimes even hiding the hen behind his outspread wings!

## Black-winged Lory—*Eos cyanogenia*

**Synonym:** Blue-cheeked Lory

**Distribution:** Found in various West Irian Islands: Biak, Manim, Numfoor, and Mios Num; and islands in the Geelvink Bay.

**Description:** The ground color is a rather dull red which is wholly interwoven with violet. Most of the wing is black, but the secondaries are red. The primaries (of which the fifth has a gold patch) and thighs are black with a dull blue sheen. There is a blue "fan" running from the beak through the eyes to the shoulders, neck, and nape. The central tail feathers are black, the outer feathers are red with black edges. The undertail coverts are red. The beak is orange, the iris is reddish-brown, and

the feet are dark gray. Juveniles are similar to adults except that the red is interwoven with black-purple and the beak is black. Adult birds are robust with a plump body.

**Length:** 11.8 inches (30 cm); wings, 6.3 inches (16 cm); tail, 4.4 inches (11.5 cm).

**Habitat:** In spite of their heavy looking build, these birds are quite fast on the wing. On the ground they are also agile, more so than most other *Eos* species! They occur mainly along coastal areas in small groups where they are attracted to flowering palm and similar trees. They are quite noisy and fairly common both in the wild and in captivity.

**Aviculture:** I first got to know these birds at "Artis," the famous zoo of Amsterdam, during the mid 1960s. During the 1970s, they were especially available on the market in Holland and Belgium. The musky odor is quite strong in this species and they are thus best kept in spacious outdoor aviaries. For outdoor overwintering, the

The black-winged lory is often very aggressive when feeding its offspring. Hybrids with a female red lory were reared at the San Diego Zoo in 1972 and 1973.

57

# Lories And Lorikeets

night shelter should have mild heating to not less than 50°F (10°C). Newly imported birds must be carefully acclimatized before being placed outdoors and then the sleeping box should be placed in a light and warm spot, preferably so that the birds can sit on top of the box below a good insulated ceiling. These birds have a nerve splitting shriek, which they use mainly in the mornings. Once accustomed to a new owner and premises, they become a little quieter, though they still will scream occasionally very loudly early mornings as if they want to make their presence felt. Some neighbors may not take kindly to this noise. If you intend to keep such birds, you should make amends with the neighbors *before* you get them, rather than have difficulties later.

**Remarks:** It is not easy to determine the sexes of these birds, but with pairs I have seen, including the pair in my possession, the cock is more robust than the hen. It is a well-known fact that cock and hen lories and lorikeets are especially very affectionate toward one another; this species, however, being the exception!

These birds become tame and affectionate toward their owners; my pair takes tidbits from my fingers every day; frequently sitting on my sleeve. The hen lays two eggs, about 1.1 by 0.9 inches (29 x 24 mm), which she incubates for about 27 days; both parents feed the young that are quite slow in development. During this time, the birds can become quite aggressive toward their owner. I once had a breeding pair in a breeding cage in my bird room (which stank of the musky smell of the lories); as soon as I put my hand in the cage to inspect the nest box, both birds attacked it, pecking and biting with their beaks! Youngsters stay in the nest for a relatively long period; approximately 12 to 13½ weeks; they are fed by the parents for a further two weeks.

If the parents are about to start a new brood, it is important to remove the young from the previous brood, otherwise it is possible the cock will injure or even kill them! My best breeding results have occurred with pairs in aviaries 6 feet (2 m) long, 5½ feet (1.5 m) wide, and 6 feet (2 m) high.

## Genus *Lorius* (Broad-tailed Lories)

Formerly known as *Domicella*, this genus contains eight species and 13 to 15 subspecies, depending, of course, on whose nomenclature one follows. A characteristic of members of this genus is the somewhat plumpish body form; the short, broad, and rounded tail; and the mainly red plumage, apart from the green wings and the blue on the neck, back, head, thighs, and/or abdomen. All of the species, which range between 10.2 and 16.1 inches (26 and 41 cm) in length, have a red beak and an orange-red iris. Experience has shown that most of the species are intolerant of cold weather, drafts, and dampness, and I would strongly recommend a minimum captive temperature of 50°F (10°C). These beautiful, generally slow, and heavy flying birds need a lot of space and I therefore do not recommend cages. Roomy indoor or outdoor aviaries with a heatable protective wind, rain, and night shelter are more suitable. The concrete floor of the aviary is best covered with corncob, as the birds' droppings are loose, copious, and strong smelling. In the interests of hygiene, a natural floor is considered unsuitable.

Extra fruit and insects are eagerly accepted by these birds, and the black-capped lory (*L. l. lory*), for example, is known for its habit of catching and eating cockroaches. A choice of thick perches, 2 to 2¾ inches (5–7 cm) in diameter, should be given and, as these will be continually reduced to splinters by the birds, will have to be regularly replaced. I personally find the branches and twigs of fruit or willow trees to be the most suitable. The dimensions of the nest boxes will, of course, be dictated by the sizes of the individual species.

# *Lories And Lorikeets*

*Lorius* species are well-known for their intelligence. They quickly become tame and affectionate, and some can mimic the human voice and other sounds (the barking of a dog, for example) amazingly well. If a stranger comes too close to the cage or aviary for their liking, especially during nesting time, they are likely to create absolute bedlam! And they have the necessary voices for creating a row! The courtship behavior of these birds is very interesting to watch. The cock approaches the hen, nodding his head and making comical dancing movements, while letting out a gurgling, somewhat growling noise. Copulation takes place on a thick, stable perch; the cock places one of his feet on the hen's back and holds on to the perch with the other. Several copulations per day (sometimes prolonged as in other lories) are possible; especially with those pairs that are housed alone. These lories are aptly named "the monkeys of the bird world" and it is fun to see a pair of them locked in an embrace and rolling over on the floor of their aviary as if engaged in a serious wrestling match.

In their native lands, they are frequently collected from their nests by the local people. They are leg-ringed, usually with a small section of bone, and tethered with a chain on a stand (this is illegal in our country, and rightly so). The birds soon become tame and trusting. They also may be pinioned and kept freely around the home. Both methods are of course cruel, especially the pinioning that is frequently done on both wings in a rough manner. Of course the birds lose their power of flight forever and are sentenced to an invalid life of running about on the floor. Sometimes such birds are imported; they are usually very tame, but are no value whatsoever as aviary birds.

The birds in this genus all have a naked eyering, which is gray-colored in youngsters and black in adults. They cannot be kept together with other parrotlike birds, but usually will tolerate smaller birds (finches and quail, for example) in the aviary. All of the species love to bathe. Give them a heavy (to prevent them from dragging it about), shallow waterbath. It is an amusing sight to see the birds rolling around in the water.

## Black-capped Lory—*Lorius l. lory*

**Synonym:** Tri-colored Lory

**Distribution:** Found in West Irian, Vogelkop, Waigeu, Batanta, Salawati, and Mysol (western Papuan Islands).

**Description:** Full-colored birds have a black crown (more or less the trademark of this species), contrasting splendidly with the light red of the cheeks, throat, neck, sides of the belly, lower back, rump, and uppertail coverts. A blue-black band runs from the lower part of the neck to the throat. The thighs are blue in color, as are the breast, belly, upper back, and undertail feathers. The wings are green (olive green on the shoulders), as are the central tail feathers. The tips of

The black-capped lories are not noisy birds and perhaps therefore very popular. They are fairly willing breeders, and hand-reared chicks prove excellent mimics.

the tail feathers are dark blue. The inside of the primary wing feathers is yellow, and the underwing coverts are red. The beak is orange-yellow; the feet are gray-black, and the iris is yellow-orange.

**Length:** 12.2 inches (31 cm); wings: cock, 6.3 to 6.7 inches (16–17 cm); hen, 6 to 6.3 inches (15–16 cm); tail: cock, 3.5 to 4 inches (9–10 cm); hen, 3.2 to 3.5 inches (8–9 cm).

Young birds lack the red headband and are greenish between the shoulders. They also possess a blue ring around the neck, whereas the upper breast is red and the underwing coverts are yellow with black spots. The lesser underwing coverts are a mixture of green, blue, and red feathers, and the blue of the breast does not yet meet the neck. The red on the sides of the breast and the sides of the belly is of different shades. The iris and the beak are first brownish.

**Habitat:** Fairly common in the wild, these birds live in coastal rainforests, and inland to an altitude of about 5250 feet (1600 m). They spend most of the time in the tree canopy. Outside the breeding season they live in groups of 8 to 12, but during the breeding season they stay strictly as pairs. When the trees are in blossom or at fruiting time, several groups may converge and sometimes form flocks of several hundreds. They then make a lot of noise in the treetops, flying from one tree to another, or clambering from twig to twig like so many monkeys. Nesting holes are generally high up in a hollow tree trunk or limb.

**Aviculture:** Captive pairs quickly become tame and trusting, and usually will breed readily in a quiet, roomy indoor or outdoor aviary. They require a thick-walled nest box, which they will use all year-round for breeding and sleeping. Best dimensions for the nest box are 12 by 12 by 18 inches (30 x 30 x 45 cm), with a 3.3-inch (8-cm) diameter entrance hole. The hen lays two eggs, about 1 by 0.9 inch (27 x 22 mm), and these hatch after about 26 days. The young leave the nest in about 11 weeks but are fed by both parents for a further two weeks.

The black-capped lory is probably the best known and loved member of the brush-tongued parrot group. The stunning colors, relatively easy care, their affection, and the ease of breeding all have contributed to their popularity. A pair never should be kept together with the same or other parrotlike species—the cock especially can be very aggressive and would make short work of any other hookbeak that got in his way. During the winter the birds are best kept in heated—[59°F (15°C) or more]—accommodations, but should still have the use of a thick-walled nest box.

The species was first described in 1751 and at that time they were already popular pet birds with the island natives. Their mimical talents are not great, but some individuals will learn a few words or repeat sounds, especially the songs of other birds in the area. There are at least seven subspecies, of which the following are important in aviculture:

The **Red-breasted Lory** (*L. l. erythrothorax*) comes from the southern part of Geelvink Bay and the Onin Peninsula. **Length:** 11.8 inches (30 cm); wings: cock, 6.3 to 6.7 inches (16–17 cm); hen, 6 to 6.3 inches (15–16 cm); tail: cock, 3.5 to 4 inches (9–10 cm); hen, 3.1 to 3.5 inches (8–9 cm). This subspecies is easy to recognize by its red breast, as all other subspecies have a blue breast. The neck and shoulders are dark purplish-blue, whereas the belly, the thighs, and the undertail coverts are more violet-blue. The cheeks are red, as are the upper throat, breast, sides of the belly, flanks, upper part of the back, and uppertail coverts. The underwings are yellow with some black spots; the underwing coverts are red. Young birds have a blue belly with red feathers. In general, this subspecies is similar to the nominate form.

*L. l. somu* is similar to the foregoing subspecies. It comes from southern New Guinea. **Length:** 11.4 inches (29 cm); wings: cock, 6 to 6.3 inches (15–16 cm); hen, 5.5 to 6 inches (14–15 cm); tail: cock, 3.5 to 4 inches (9–10 cm); hen, 3.1 to 3.5 inches (8–9 cm). A character-

# *Lories And Lorikeets*

The red-breasted lories require relatively easy care. Their affection and easy breeding have contributed to their popularity.

istic of this form is the absence of the blue neck band.

*L. l. salvadorii*, in contrast, has a conspicuous blue neck band, and the underside of the wings is dark blue. It comes from the northern part of New Guinea. **Length:** 11.8 inches (30 cm); wings, 6.3 to 6.7 inches (16–17 cm); tail, 3.5 to 4 inches (9–10 cm).

The **Jobi Lory** (*L. l. jobiensis*), as its name implies, comes from Jobi and Mios Num, small islands in Geelvink Bay. The bird is similar to the nominate form. **Length:** 11.8 inches (30 cm); wings, 6.7 inches (17 cm); tail, 4 inches (10 cm). The underwing coverts are blue and black, whereas the other feathers under the wings are purplish-black. The red on the body of this species is more rosy-red. The belly is blue in adults; mixed with green in youngsters. The sexes of adults are relatively easy to distinguish, especially if you have several specimens to compare: males

have a deep blue neck band and deep blue undertail coverts; whereas these parts are light blue in the females. A healthy male weighs about 9.7 ounces (275 g); a female about 7.8 ounces (220 g). These birds love to eat mealworms and cockroaches. They are regularly available and are sometimes offered as black-capped lories—so always carefully check out what you buy.

## Purple-naped Lory — *Lorius domicellus*

**Synonym:** Purple-capped Lory

**Distribution:** Found in Oram and Amboina (Indonesia). In the last century, the species was introduced to the island of Buru.

**Description:** This species is easy to recognize by its yellow breast band that runs over the line of the crop; most of the body is carmine red. The top of the head is black, with a violet shimmer toward the back; the wings are olive-green, as are the wing coverts. The primary wing feathers are dark green; black at the ends. There is a blue band on the wings and the undertail coverts are more or less blue. The tail is red above with a light red tip; the underside of the tail is goldish-red. The underwing coverts are bluish-green and the inside of the primaries are yellow. The thighs are blue, the beak is orange-red, the iris is dark brown with a yellow inner ring, and the feet are black. The yellow breast band varies in size from individual to individual; youngsters can be recognized by the green feathers on the shoulders.

**Length:** 11 inches (28 cm); wings, 6.3 to 6.7 inches (16–17 cm); tail, 3.5 to 4 inches (9–10 cm).

**Habitat:** I have observed this species in Amboina always in pairs. They live mostly in wooded areas but I also have seen them in parks and larger gardens. They are very boisterous in their manner. They breed usually in hollow tree trunks, but I also have seen the nests in thick, hollow branches. The eggs average about 1.3 by 1 inch (32 x 25.5 mm). The islanders frequently keep these colorful and charming birds as pets. I have seen many children

# *Lories And Lorikeets*

The purple-naped lory is an excellent breeder; however, the nesting period could be very variable: depending on menu and temperature it ranges between 7 and 14 weeks.

going off to school with one or more of the birds perched on their shoulders. Some years ago this species was frequently exported (it was first seen in Europe, in Holland, in 1751, but the first record of the bird in England is from 1872). Unfortunately, the pressure of export coupled with loss of habitat through forest clearance has made the species much scarcer and it is now only occasionally available in the trade. I have seen these birds in aviaries in many Indonesian hotels and restaurants, where their brilliant colors and clownlike behavior attract much attention.

**Aviculture:** I have kept a number of pairs at various times over the years. They are very fond of dehusked sunflower seeds and all kinds of fruit. With their remarkable inquisitiveness, they soon become very tame and trusting. One of my birds always came directly to the wire when I approached the aviary, and followed me screeching to the aviary door where he sat still on the wire. In

order to prevent his escape, I had to attract his attention by pushing a few grapes through the aviary wire. This soon became a daily habit, and if I ever forget the grapes I was soon screechingly reprimanded! Pairs are best kept to themselves, at least without other members of the same species or other parrotlike birds. Small finches or similar birds are probably okay, but I always prefer to keep my pairs on their own.

On introduction, the cocks can, at first, be aggressive toward the hens, but after a few weeks they will behave as a loving pair. A large birch nesting log is ideal for this species. Two eggs are laid and the downy-white young hatch after about 26 days. Only the hen incubates the eggs. During the breeding period, the cock will get quite irritable and sometimes aggressive—so watch out when you enter the aviary. At about 16 days of age, the white down on the young gradually will be changing to gray. At about four weeks after hatching, the first feathers appear and the eyes begin to open. The young leave the nest at about 12 weeks. These birds should never be kept below 50°F (10°C) and it is best to house them in an indoor aviary with thick perches, at normal room temperature during the winter.

## Chattering Lory—*Lorius g. garrulus*

**Distribution:** Found in Halmahera and the Weda Islands.

**Description:** This species is mainly bright red in color, with the exception of the olive-green wings; the bend of the wing is yellow as are the underwing coverts. The inside of the wing primaries is red. The upper base of the tail is red,

Top left: The "normal" form of the Stella's lorikeet.
Top right: In the wild, the melanistic form of the Stella's lorikeet is three to four times more numerous.
Bottom: Fairy lorikeet.

# *Lories And Lorikeets*

The chattering lory is one of the best-known lories in aviculture. It is easily managed, hardy, and will breed frequently. The parents, however, are often aggressive when their young are present.

merging into dark purple and ending with a green tinge. The underside of the tail is a golden-red. The iris is yellow-orange; in the cock bird the pupil has a narrow white edge; this is gray in the hen. The eye-ring is purplish-black, the beak is orange-red, and the feet are gray-black.

**Length:** 11.8 inches (30 cm); wings, 6.7 to 7.1 inches (17–18 cm); tail, 4 inches (10 cm). The young are duller in color, with a blackish-brown beak. The eyes are dark. They reach full adult coloration at about six months of age, and

Top: Dusky lory.
Bottom left: Musschenbroek's lorikeet.
Bottom right: The purple-crowned lorikeet is known for its short incubation time (17-18 days). This "Aussie" is extremely rare in aviculture.

sexes can be distinguished by weight in that the hen is a good 1 to 1.8 ounces (30–50 g) lighter than the cock. The hen's head is also somewhat narrower and smaller in build.

**Habitat:** These birds are quite common in their native habitat, and they frequently are kept by the locals as pets. In the wild they travel about in pairs and they can be quite quarrelsome with other members of their own species, especially in feeding trees where the food supply is not too great and birds have to rely on their strength to get the most food. Each pair has its own territory, which it vigorously defends, especially if it contains good feeding areas. They breed in hollow limbs of usually dead trees; the hen lays two eggs, about 1 by 0.9 inch (26 x 22 mm), that are incubated for 28 days. The young fledge at 70 to 80 days. The breeding season usually falls in June, but the young are fed by the parents until late in the year; I have seen birds still feeding their young in November!

**Aviculture:** These birds are best kept in single pairs, but they can be kept together with other birds in aviaries as long as there are not other parrotlike birds! Occasionally you get a lory that is aggressive toward *all* other birds in the aviary and, in such cases, it is of course best to leave the other birds out of the scheme of things. In spite of this, I would recommend the chattering lory as an ideal species for the beginner to loriculture; not only are they relatively inexpensive, they soon become extremely tame, and as affectionate as a dog! When purchasing these birds, make sure they are not pinioned—a mutilation that must be strongly condemned! Also, watch out for so-called "differences in colors between sexes." I have seen several "pairs" of chattering lories that are two different subspecies and the owner thought that the different sizes of the yellow patches on the wings was a difference between sexes! In fact, a cock and a hen of the same subspecies have very little, if any, color differences, and especially not in the yellow patches. The only sex difference of

# *Lories And Lorikeets*

importance is that the cock is somewhat more robust in form than the hen.

**Remarks:** This is one of the hardiest and most frequently imported species and with optimum care soon will be breeding. Give them a good lory diet, some willow twigs, a little birdseed and unripe weed seeds, and a few endive leaves every day. A large aviary will not be necessary. With a well-insulated night shelter and a thick-walled nest box, this species can be kept in an outdoor aviary all year round. It is truly an amazing sight to see these birds gambolling around in the snow. They are extremely playful birds, that do not often let out their nerve-grating shrieks, but are capable of mimicking a range of other sounds; especially whistling. Some can learn to repeat a few words. Most birds I have had became tame in a few weeks and would sit on my head or shoulder without any sign of fear. If I walked past the aviary without giving them a treat, they would scream out and continue to do so until they received the attention they required. When they have eggs or young in the nest, they are very aggressive. I frequently had to wear gloves and carry a net to keep them at bay when I entered the aviary in order to inspect the nest. Do not be too worried if the hen should appear to leave the eggs for too long in order to snatch some air. After feeding and sometimes bathing, she often will return to the nest with soaking wet plumage. But it is surprising how long the eggs stay warm; at first I was quite worried myself until I realized that the eggs still felt warm even after 45 minutes. Young chattering lories fledge at eight to ten weeks but are still fed by the parents for some time after. As soon as the parents are ready to start on their next brood, the youngsters must be removed to their own quarters, as there is a chance that the male, especially, will injure or even kill his offspring.

Unfortunately these birds often look a bit scruffy in pet stores because they are not given the opportunity to bathe, nor do they get a lukewarm spray. They must have a daily opportunity to bathe if their plumage is to stay in top condition.

There is one subspecies that is important in aviculture: the yellow-backed lory (*L. g. flavopalliatus*) comes from the Moluccan islands of Morotai, Raou, Batjan, and Obi, and differs from the nominate form in having a large yellow patch on its back, filling up the area between the shoulders. The green on the wings is also deeper in color.

**Length:** 11.8 inches (30 cm); wings, 6.7 to 7.1 inches (17–18 cm); tail, 4 to 4.3 inches (10-11 cm). Unfortunately the bird market often offers two subspecies as a "pair" and this is naturally not right! But regular good breeding results are reported. This subspecies—in my view—is more colorful than the nominate form and is popular both in England and the United States. Care is similar to that of the nominate form. The first captive breeding took place in England around 1958. The birds are known for their aggression before and during the breeding season (in my view even more so than the nominate form) and breeders often have difficulty in entering the aviary. In addition to the normal lory menu, one should offer a variety of fruit and a good brand of egg food (CéDé, L/M Universal Plus), boiled potato (!), and a good ration of mealworms. The mealworms should be killed first, as living mealworms can damage the inside of the gut and even "bite themselves out." Put the mealworms in an old nylon stocking and hold them in boiling water for 20 seconds or so.

Some fanciers recommend spraying lukewarm water on the eggs (preferably with a plant sprayer) just before they hatch, as the hen does not like to leave the eggs at hatching time. This should help make the hatching a little easier.

Youngsters should be moved to separate quarters the moment they are independently feeding for the same reasons as mentioned for the nominate form.

66

# *Lories And Lorikeets*

## Genus *Phigys* (Solitary Lories)

This genus contains just a single species; a small bird with an elongated red and green neck and mantle feathers. The body is relatively slight and the tail is short. They occur on various islands in the Fiji group. Although they always have been prized avicultural specimens, they are quite scarce in captivity. However, they are still to be seen in the better bird and zoological gardens and in the hands of some private fanciers, especially in California, Belgium, and the Netherlands. They are still quite common in some parts of their native range, in spite of enemies in the form of egg and nestling collectors (see page 68). There are some subspecies, but these are to my knowledge never offered for sale on the general market. This genus is very similar to the genus *Vini* (see page 68). The genus *Phigys* was formerly known as *Calliptilus*.

## Collared Lory—*Phigys solitarius*

**Synonyms:** Solitary Lory, Fiji Lory, or Ruffled Lory

**Distribution:** Found in Fiji Islands. In spite of the specific name, these birds are not particularly solitary in their habits and often forage in pairs or small groups.

**Description:** The throat, breast, belly, and most of the cheeks are red. Its back, wings, and tail are green, the rump is light green. The neck band is red, and the crown, thighs, and rear part of the body are black-violet. The underwing coverts and undertail feathers are green, the latter with orange flecks. The beak is orange-yellow, the iris is reddish-brown, and the feet are flesh-colored.

**Length:** 7.5 inches (19 cm); wings, 5.1 inches (13 cm); tail, 2.6 inches (6.5 cm). The hen has a dull indigo-blue forehead, and greenish feathers on the back of the crown. The hen is usually somewhat slighter in build, with a rounder and smaller head. The young have yellow flecks in the purple of the breast, whereas the beak is still light gray-brown, the iris is dark brown-black, and the feet are gray.

**Habitat:** The birds are ever foraging in blooming trees and, according to Forshaw, especially in coconut palms, drala (*Erythrina indica*), and African tulip. The flight is quick and straight, without the usual undulations; they emit a continual, shrill, two-note screech during flight. They have the habit of landing on the outer twigs of trees and with hopping motions make their way "deeper" into the foliage in search of blossoms or fruits. These birds are different from most other lories and lorikeets in that they often nest in a hollow trunk quite close to the ground and thus are susceptible to attacks by rats that kill and eat the eggs and young. On some islands the local government has introduced mongooses (ferretlike mammals) in order to combat the rats but, sadly, mongooses themselves find the young of lorikeets somewhat

The collared lory is an island species that is still abundant. It is one of the most beautiful birds among the little lories!

# *Lories And Lorikeets*

delectable! The islanders often collect young birds and raise them as household pets or sell them.

**Aviculture:** The first collared lory arrived in England in 1870, but they have always been relatively scarce in the aviculture. The first reported breeding took place in the aviaries of the English breeder Lord Tavistock in 1939. The well-known Swiss aviculturist, Dr. R. Burhard, has raised five generations of the birds from various pairs since 1968! The hen lays two eggs, about 1 by 0.8 inch (25.5 x 20 mm), but usually only one youngster reaches fledging age! The incubation period is about 28 days and the young leave the nest when they are about 64 days old. In the aviary, adult birds (best kept in single pairs) are very active and comical, continually clambering around the perches and wire and performing endless acrobatics. However, this species is not the easiest to acclimatize to captive life and diet. One of the first requirements is that acclimatized birds should have the daily use of fresh bathwater. They love to bathe. Newly imported birds should be kept at a minimum temperature of 68°F (20°C) and definitely not lower. They are particularly susceptible to aspergillosis and candidiasis. Give a supplement of vitamin A and, in cooperation with your veterinarian, give chlorhexadine (Nolvasan, for example) in the drinking water. These birds prefer deep, dark nest boxes in which they will sleep at night and also breed. They are not suited to cages, and should be kept in a roomy indoor aviary or an outdoor aviary with a weatherproof night shelter where the nest box should be placed, in such a manner that there is room for the cock to sit on the top of it.

In addition to the food diet recommended for broad-tailed lories (*Lorius*), they like egg food (commercial egg food is okay) and rusks. The best breeding results occur when these birds are kept in groups (eight to ten pairs) together in a large outdoor aviary. Fortunately they do not have a loud or unpleasant voice. In captivity these birds incubate for 28 days, sometimes a day or two longer, depending on the outdoor temperature. The first red and green feathers appear on the young when they are about 20 to 21 days old and a week later the head is fully covered with feathers. At about nine weeks of age, they leave the nest. In addition to mashed fruit, the parents will feed honey, soft apple, and baby food to the youngsters, as well as the mixture suggested on page 25, to which I like to add ant pupae and grated carrot. Fanciers of this species are all convinced that they are the most attractive of all the lories; Sydney Porter, the famous ornithologist, himself has said that they are "the loveliest and most engaging of the whole Parrot tribe!"

# Genus *Vini* (Virgin or Fringe Parrots)

These small, interesting birds are mainly green and blue colored, with short tails (the middle feathers are longer than the outer ones) and, especially, the long neck feathers that probably play a part in courtship. The beak is relatively small (smaller than the foregoing species). They feed largely on nectar and soft, juicy fruits. In the wild they spend much time in the crowns of coconut palms, hiding there in times of danger. They will nest in coconuts that have been gnawed by rats and have dried out but are still affixed to the stem. These lories sometimes move from one island to another; the inhabitants of these islands, who are becoming ever less isolated through the modern air and sea transport, catch these birds with the help of a coconut fiber noose that is affixed to a long stick. Another tame bird, sitting on a bamboo pole, attracts wild birds with its call. As soon as a wild bird lands on the stick with the noose (which is next to the bamboo pole), the noose is pulled tight. The birds are fed on coconut flesh and sugar water.

# Lories And Lorikeets

Because these are real tropical birds, they must be kept in lightly heated aviaries and can spend only the warmer summer months in outdoor aviaries.

The diet consists mainly of the usual lory food (see page 25), that should, however, not be made too heavy as it can cause liver problems—dilute with water. Soft, juicy fruits, ant pupae, and chopped mealworms also can be offered regularly. They are very fond of apples—as are the preceding species! This species will breed in captivity, though they cannot be considered "easy." Egg binding is common at lower temperatures. The nest box should (see preceding species) also be deep. Line the inside with slabs of turf and provide a layer of wood pulp. A high humidity is important; 80 percent is recommended. Both sexes incubate the eggs and the cock broods the hatchlings while the hen forages for food. Virgin lories are very active, fly well, and quarrel a lot even with their own mates! Five species are recognized in the genus but the only one that occasionally appears on the market, and is bred mainly in California and Germany is the Tahiti blue lory.

## Tahiti Blue Lory—*Vini peruviana* (formerly known as *V. cyanea* and *V. taitana*)

**Synonym:** White-throated Lory and Indigo Lory

**Distribution:** Found in the Cook and Society Islands, and the westernmost islands of the Tuamotu group (Low/Forshaw). Attempts were made during the 1930s to reintroduce the species to Tahiti, but this was not a success (no doubt due to the rats!). As these beautiful, white and indigo birds (regarded by some as the most attractive of all parrots) are so widely distributed about the islands, it is difficult to estimate their present status. Due to the current scarce and irregular reports of sightings, it cannot be ruled out that the birds are in grave danger of extinction! All captive birds must therefore be monitored, so that maximum captive breeding is achieved and the species can perhaps thus be saved from extinction. Perhaps only wishful thinking on my part? With the small numbers of birds in captivity, every encouragement to breed should be given by making sure that they have the right conditions. It would not be the first time that aviculture has saved a particular species.

**Description:** The plumage is mainly dark indigo-blue to dark blue, whereas the cheeks and throat are white. The primary wing feathers and the tail are black, the outer edges are dark blue. The beak and the feet are brownish-orange. The white of the cheeks and throat is at first gray-black in the youngsters. The hen is usually (with sufficient comparative material) recognizable from the lighter brown colored and narrower beak, and a slightly smaller head.

The Tahiti blue lory is an unusual little parrot. It has violet-blue plumage and sturdy legs and feet.

# *Lories And Lorikeets*

**Length:** 7.1 inches (18 cm); wings, 4.3 inches (11 cm); tail, 2.4 to 2.8 inches (6–7 cm).

**Habitat:** Little is known about the wild habitat of these birds. With recent visits to the islands by various ornithologists, it seems that they are very rare. They probably breed in hollow limbs high up in the trees or in rotten coconuts. They spend a lot of time high up in the crowns of coconut palms where they are continually clambering around. The call is a soft chirp and an occasional several note call.

**Aviculture:** As far as is known, the first birds were imported into Europe (England and Belgium) in 1936 and the famous English aviculturist Lord Tavistock bred them in the next year; one of the two young being successfully raised. A later brood produced two young; the normal number per clutch. Both cock and hen share in the incubation. In 1977, a few pairs were smuggled into the United States and were confiscated by the customs and placed in the San Diego Zoo. In 1978, a youngster was born, but later died. In 1979, the breeding was more successful and two young were reared from one pair.

Incubation takes 21 to 24 days. The hen mainly looks after the young, whereas the cock stays in the area of the nest. The young fledge at about 60 days. The main diet is a thin solution of honey (see page 25), mixed with baby food, berries, apple, grapes, and ant pupae; also small mealworms—provided in an open dish—will be eaten by the parents as well as offered to the young. They are also very fond of pomegranates!

It is essential to keep these lories warm; the temperature should not drop below 68°F (20°C). They love to bathe and, if kept in outdoor aviaries, they love to take a shower in the summer rain. There have been breeding successes in Europe, going by the advertisements in the (especially German) avicultural magazines, offering them for sale.

## Genus *Charmosyna* (Ornamental or Honey Lories)

Ornamental or honey lories are small to medium-sized, elegantly built birds that are instantly recognizable by their pointed tails that in some species are longer, in others shorter, than the wings. The beak is always red, and many species are very colorful, with red, green, yellow, and blue to purple as the main colors. Fourteen species and 11 subspecies are currently recognized. Those with a melanistic color are recognized as subspecies.

Diet consists mainly of nectar and pollen, but all kinds of fruit may be taken. The larger species also eat seeds, and all more or less take insects. Larger species should not be kept below 50°F (10°C); small species not below 68°F (20°C).

There is an easily recognizable sexual dimorphism and the tongue is somewhat longer than in any other lories and lorikeets; they can in fact lick their eyes with the tongue, which they do when they are wet with fruit juices. These birds are susceptible to aspergillosis and candidiasis and newly imported specimens must be acclimatized with the greatest of care; especially with regard to diet and temperature. It is sometimes thought that because these birds live in the mountains that they can tolerate lower temperatures; but this does not mean they will be comfortable in our winters! Newly imported birds should be kept at least at room temperature. In states with very cold winters, they never should be placed in outdoor aviaries unless they have a heated night shelter. Newly acquired birds should be offered soft fruits and honey/glucose solution with added vitamin preparation. As these birds feed more with their tongue than most lories, it is important that their diet is quite fluid so that they easily can take it up.

## Fairy Lorikeet—
### *Charmosyna p. pulchella*

**Synonym:** Fair Lorikeet

**Distribution:** Found in the mountains of western New Guinea.

**Description:** This species is easy to recognize by the brilliant red of the plumage that is broken by the black-green back and wings and the blackish rump. The breast and thighs are striped yellow. The forehead is red and the back of the head is violet-black, edged with a blue neck band; the center of the belly may sometimes be violet colored; the tail feathers are red at the base, green edged, and yellow tipped. The very long central tail feathers are wholly red, with orange red tips. The hen has a yellow patch instead of red on each side of the violet belly. Her body is more slender and slighter than that of the cock.

**Length:** 7.1 to 7.5 inches (18–19 cm); wings, 3.7 inches (9.5 cm); tail, 3.6 inches (9.2 cm). The young have a greenish wash over the whole plumage; the beak, iris, and feet are dark brown.

**Habitat:** These birds occur at 6570 feet (2000 m) altitude in the mountains so it is not surprising

The fairy lorikeet is rather well known in aviculture. The bird's bill and nails grow quickly and therefore require constant attention.

that little is known about their wild habits. They usually live in pairs or small groups, sometimes together with other lory species. They have a straight and fast flight path. They feed on nectar and pollen, plus many small insects that occur on the flowers and leaves. While feeding and while on the wing, they continually emit their shrill, piping call. The breeding season falls during the time of winter in the United States.

**Aviculture:** The first specimens arrived in Europe (Scotland) in 1914, but it was only in the 1970s that more recent specimens arrived in Germany and England although, unfortunately, there were more hens than cocks in these consignments. They are best kept together in single pairs. Breeding successes have been reported in indoor aviaries and large cages with minimal dimensions of 4 feet (120 cm) long by 19½ inches (50 cm) wide by 24 inches (60 cm) high and even in a smaller 19½ by 15¾ by 11¾ inches (50 x 40 x 30 cm) cage with a budgerigar nest box affixed outside the cage.

Usually two eggs, about 0.8 by 0.6 inch (18.9 x 16.2 mm), are laid, and these are incubated for 25 days. The cock frequently accompanies the hen in the nest, but whether he actually incubates has not been ascertained. Young birds have at first white, later somewhat gray, down. They open the eyes at 20 to 22 days and leave the nest at about two months.

My general impressions and experience with this species, which is not much bigger and more slender than a budgie, have shown that it requires very careful acclimatization. They really should be acquired only by experienced fanciers, as they tend to be difficult captives. I have personally discovered that they prefer a very fluid diet. I give my birds daily a dish with a very fluid solution of honey, which they take readily, and I mix in a little *Lactobacillus acidophilus* and this seems to help prevent any sudden illnesses.

There are two subspecies, namely the Rothschild's fairy lorikeet (*C. p. rothschildi*) from the mountains of northern New Guinea, and *C. p. bella* from the mountains of central and eastern New Guinea. The latter subspecies is somewhat doubtfully placed and could be a synonym of *C. p. pulchella*. They generally resemble the nominate form. In both subspecies there is marked sexual dimorphism; the hen has a yellowish green lower back, which is red in the cock. The Rothschild's fairy lorikeet is somewhat larger than the nominate form, 7½ inches (19 cm), for the cock; the hens are somewhat shorter and slighter in build. Some pairs were imported into Germany and England in 1973; they require similar care to the nominate form.

## Josephine's Lorikeet—*C. j. josefinae*

**Distribution:** Found in the mountains of western New Guinea (Vogelkop to the Snow Mountains).

**Description:** This species is like a miniature version of the Stella's lorikeet (*C. papou stellae*). The main color is red, with a green back and wings. The back of the head is black with a violet patch that runs through to the eye. The belly and flanks are a velvety black. The rump is blue. The central tail feathers are dark red with yellow tips; the remainder are red at the base grayish-green on the edges and orange-yellow towards the tips. The beak, iris, and feet are orange-red. The lower back in the cock is red; in the hen, it is yellow with a soft green shimmer.

**Length:** 9.6 inches (24.5 cm); wings, 5 inches (12.5 cm); tail, 5.1 inches (13 cm). The hen has a slighter build.

**Habitat:** This species occurs to an altitude of 6570 feet (2000 m) in the coastal ranges, usually in pairs or in groups of four to six pairs, sometimes in the company with fairy lorikeets. Like the fairy lorikeets, their diet consists of nectar, pollen, tiny insects, and small juicy fruits. They are capable of emitting a somewhat unpleasant

screech but, in general, can be regarded as reasonably quiet birds.

**Aviculture:** These birds frequently are imported in bad condition. They require careful acclimatization and I would recommend the species only to experienced fanciers. During courtship, the cock approaches the hen with outspread tail and nodding head. This is very interesting and amusing to observe, but keep your distance and use binoculars if necessary as you will otherwise disturb them. The two eggs, about 10.9 by 0.7 inch (23 x 17 mm), are incubated by the hen for about 28 days; the cock often spends time with her on the nest, though probably does not directly incubate. The young hatch with white down that changes to gray in about two weeks. The eyes open in 21 to 22 days and the first feathers also appear at this time. They leave the nest at 35 to 37 days of age.

## Stella's Lorikeet—*C. papou stellae*

**Distribution:** Found in the mountains of southeastern New Guinea.

**Description:** The cock is very similarly colored to the nominate form (see above). The essential visible differences are: 1. The patch on the crown and neck is, in this subspecies, larger, is deep purple-blue with a whitish sheen, and marked with a black band. 2. All yellow on the body is absent. The wings and the thighs are dark green. There is some yellow on the hen; the hen is somewhat slighter in build than the cock. The young also have yellow markings at first; also a red tail and a brown beak.

**Length:** 16.5 inches (42 cm); wings, 5.7 inches (14.5 cm); tail, 10 inches (25 cm). This subspecies also occurs in melanistic form (see illustration on page 63), that is dominant over the red. It seems that most of these black birds are cocks and my colleague F. Beswerda of the Netherlands says that "it is interesting to note that where these birds occur the people say that two

# *Lories And Lorikeets*

Stella's lorikeet makes an excellent pet.

black individuals never pair up, but always a black with a 'normal' red bird." It seems that there are more of the black birds at the higher altitudes of their range at 200 to 850 feet (2500–3000 m).

**Habitat:** Similar to that of the nominate form.

**Aviculture:** This subspecies has been known in aviculture since about 1900 and the first reported breeding was in Scotland in 1910. At the end of 1970, a number of these birds became available in Europe (especially) and the United States. They are ideal aviary subjects, that do well together with some of the larger softbills (tanagers, pittas). The well-known German lory expert Theo Pagel has good experience of this. These birds must have daily fresh bathwater, which they will use a lot. They must not, of course, be kept together with other parrotlike birds unless you want bloody results! They will do well on the usual lory diet (see page 25) plus a rich variety of fresh fruit.

## Genus *Hypocharmosyna* (Beautiful Lories)

Of the ten species and about 17 subspecies, only the two species (with the subspecies *ornata*) below are irregularly available in the trade. The genus chiefly contains small, charming birds that are mainly green in color and have a very similar life-style to members of the genus *Charmosyna* (see page 70) from which they were only recently moved. The normal lory diet (see page 25) can be mixed with a little yogurt, pollen meal, and vitamins (especially vitamin A). They must also have a variety of soft fruits and insects, such as mealworms, ant pupae, and enchytrae (whiteworms), the variety being especially important during the breeding season. I have had best results with single pairs in roomy indoor or outdoor aviaries. The temperature should not fall below room temperature day or night and the relative humidity should remain around 75 percent; in those states where the winters are extremely severe, the birds kept in outdoor aviaries *must* have a heated night shelter and you must make sure that the birds use it at night. There are several reports about these birds being bred in cages of 47 by 15¾ by 15¾ inches (120 x 40 x 40 cm), but in my experience I find these unsuitable, and I prefer to give my birds plenty of "lebensraum." It is interesting to note that the Wilhelmina Lorikeet (*H. wilhelminae*), from the Arfak Mountain region of West Irian, the Huon Peninsula, and part of south eastern New Guinea is the smallest lory, with a total length of just 5.1 inches (13 cm)! As far as I know this species was imported to England in 1909, but since then no records of captive specimens are available.

## Red-flanked Lorikeet —*H. p. placentis*

**Synonym:** Pleasing Lorikeet

**Distribution:** Found in Pandjang, Ceram, Amboina, Ambelau (Moluccas), and the Aru Islands.

**Description:** It is predominantly green, lighter to yellow-green on the underside. The crown is also yellow-green. The cheeks, underwing coverts, and sides of the breast are red. The ear coverts, the lower part of the back, and the rump are ultramarine blue. The tail feathers, with the exception of the central ones, are red at the base, and yellow at the tip with a black band just before the tip. The beak is orange-red. In the hen, the cheeks, the underwing coverts, and the sides of the breast are yellowish-green. The area around the ear is yellow-striped, making it easy to determine the sexes.

**Length:** 6.7 inches (17 cm); wings, 3.1 inches (8 cm); tail, 2.6 inches (6.5 cm).

**Habitat:** The birds occur, sometimes in quite large flocks, mainly in woodland and savannah, frequently close to human settlements. They can cause serious damage to coconut plantations and flowering coral trees (*Erythrina indica*). Their diet is chiefly pollen and nectar, sweet fruit, insects, leaves, buds, and fresh twigs. According to the (scarce) available literature, the nest is often a burrow in an arboreal termite mound; similar to that known for the Australian hooded parakeet (*Psephotus chrysopterygius dissimilis*). The hen lays two white eggs, about 0.8 by 0.7 inch (19 x 17.3 mm), that hatch after 22 to 23 days of incubation. The young start with white down and the eyes open at 13 to 15 days. At this time the down will have thickened and changed to gray. The young leave the nest at about two months of age, but the parents continue to feed them for another week or two. With this species, serious incubation starts after the second egg has been laid; that is the full clutch. The period between the first and second egg laying is two to four days. The voice is a shrill shriek that cannot be described as attractive.

**Aviculture:** This species has been known in aviculture for about 90 years, but the first breeding results were reported only in the 1970s. Care and breeding are very similar to that described for ornamental lories (see genus *Charmosyna*, page 70). In order to avoid candidiasis (all members of this and the preceding genus are very susceptible to the disease) as much as possible, it is recommended that extra vitamin A, together with a *Lactobacillus* preparation is offered in order to reestablish the normal intestinal flora. This can all be mixed in with the lory diet. One should always make sure that no bad or moldy food is left in the cage or aviary.

The subspecies *H. p ornata* is similar to the nominate form, with exception of the green in the back and the wing coverts that are dark green instead of light green; the blue rump patch is larger and there is a larger red patch under the eye that runs down to the throat. This subspecies comes from New Guinea (excepting the island of Gebe, and northwestern New Guinea). The birds seem to do best at a temperature of 77°F (25°C) and a relative humidity of about 75 percent. Like the nominate form, they easily will accept a "commercial" budgerigar nest box to use for sleeping and breeding. (See also habitat for nominate form.) Length: 6.7 inches (17 cm); wings, 3.3 inches (8.5 cm); tail, 2.8 inches (7 cm).

## Striated Lorikeet —*H. multistriata*

**Synonym:** Many-striped Lorikeet

**Distribution:** Found in Western New Guinea (Snow Mountains near the Fly River).

**Description:** It is mainly green; the forehead, sides of the head, and the breast are yellow with a green sheen. The back of the head is dark olive-

# Lories And Lorikeets

brown, with yellow-orange stripes on the neck. The lower part of the breast is dark green with numerous yellow stripes. The ventral area is red. The upper side of the tail is olive-green with yellowish-white tips and with red marks on the base; the underside of the tail is olive-yellow. The beak is grayish at the base, whereas the tip is orange. The iris is red and the feet are bluish-gray. Cock and hen are difficult to differentiate. The juveniles are somewhat duller in color than the adults, and they have orange-yellow spots on the nape. The stripes on the underside are only vaguely discernible.

**Length:** 7.5 inches (19 cm); wings, 3.7 inches (9.5 cm); tail, 3.7 inches (9.5 cm).

**Habitat:** This species comes from a relatively small area at altitudes between 660 and 5000 feet (200 and 1800 m). During a study trip to the area in 1984, it took me one and a half days before I found a small group of six pairs that I could view from close by. Their shrill calls had given me their position. As soon as they noticed my presence, they flew up with loud shrieks and with a great curving flight path disappeared into the woods.

**Aviculture:** At the present time, this species is regularly available. As far as I know, the first captive breeding and rearing took place in 1982 in the aviaries of W. F. P. Ross of Vessem, Netherlands. The single youngster was hand-tame and was a great attraction at many shows. (Care and management are as described for ornamental lories, see page 70.)

## Genus *Neopsittacus* (Mountain Lories)

Species in this genus are known for the well-developed gizzard, which indicates that a large amount of seed is taken in the diet. The Musschenbroek's lorikeet (*N. musschenbroekii*) is one of the first lories I ever kept; one of my pairs has been in my possession for nine years and is still in first class health. This is a middle-sized species that is very active and can be aggressive toward its keeper. Even pairs can be quite quarrelsome together. They are, however, really splendid birds with an attractive color pattern. After a few months in an aviary, they become somewhat quieter (they can—believe me—make an incredible fuss if they are scared, or if something upsets them). There are two species and six subspecies recognized; all are mountain dwellers. In their native land (New Guinea), they occur to an altitude of 6600 feet (2000 m). In the wild, they consume many unripe and ripe grass and weed seeds as well as the usual nectar and pollen. The strongly hooked beak is, in contrast to the size of the body (which reminds me of a canary that has grown out of its clothes!), remarkably large and robust. I have had varying breeding successes with this species and find them fairly easy to keep and breed even for relative beginners to the hobby.

## Musschenbroek's Lorikeet— *N. musschenbroekii*

**Distribution:** Found in the mountains of western New Guinea (Vogelkop).

**Description:** Ground color is olive brown, lighter on the underside. The crown and neck are golden-brown, with a dull yellow checkered pattern. The cheeks are light green, with numerous yellow stripes. The breast has a large, irregular-edged red patch that runs in parts almost to the flanks and is different in shape from one bird to the next. In some birds the whole breast may be covered, in others the red patch is not much bigger than 1 to 1.6 inches (2.5 to 4 cm). One should also not imagine that birds with big red patches are cocks and those with small patches are hens! The whole underside of the wing coverts, and a wide band that runs over the underside of the pri-

# Lories And Lorikeets

Musschenbroek's lorikeet loves millet spray and other small seeds.

maries are red. The upper side of the tail is green, the underside orange-yellow with red markings on the base of the outer tail feathers. The broad, robust beak is yellow-horn colored; the iris is red, and the feet are gray.

**Length:** 8 inches (20 cm); wings, 4.3 inches (11 cm); tail, 3.3 inches (8.5 cm). The juvenilies are usually duller in color, and green spots may be seen in the red breast patch. The iris and the beak are still dark brownish-black.

**Habitat:** This mountain dweller reaches an altitude of 6600 feet (2000 m) and is frequently in the company of other lory species. I have been able to observe them in the wild and quickly came to the conclusion that they spend most of the time in the lower tree canopy and leave the tree crowns to other nectar and pollen feeding species. They are fast on the wing and have a good reputation as climbers (in which they use the beak as a "third foot"). In addition to a regular lory diet, they will

eat much seed and fruit. In the wild I was able to see them taking many buds of both flowers and leaves, and small, young twigs from which they removed the bark and ate it. They continually emit a shrill call, both while feeding and in flight.

**Aviculture:** It seems the first pair of these birds was brought to England in 1933 by the English aviculturist H. Whitley. The first captive breeding successes are attributed to Sir Edward Hallstrom in Australia during the 1940s. At the present time, they are popular in the Netherlands, Belgium, Denmark, and Germany, and I did not find it difficult to get good pairs in the middle 1980s. Successful breedings are not uncommon. My birds are on a seed menu consisting of various millets, canary grass seed, some hemp, black (oil) sunflower seeds (feed sparingly as the birds will otherwise get too fat), oat groats, rape seed, wheat, and buckwheat (not really a seed but a fruit). They love a millet spray, and I am not exaggerating to say they will take this as their main seed; they will clean up a millet spray in no time at all. They also get a rich variety of fresh fruit (especially pieces of peeled sweet apples) and green food (dandelion leaves, spinach, and so on, and little willow twigs are also popular!). It is a shame that these birds always stay somewhat shy, and as you approach they quickly disappear into the nest box. I have a "widower" cock that I keep without a nest box in a large cage, 47 by 19½ by 19½ inches (120 x 50 x 50 cm). He sleeps at night on a high perch, or sometimes hanging from the cage wire.

Timber cages or aviaries are not recommended for these birds as any wood is soon destroyed by their strong beaks. However, in my experience, they usually leave their nest box in one piece. As indicated earlier, the birds will disappear into their nest box if disturbed. When peace reigns, the cock will first stick his head out of the entrance hole in order to check out the situation. If everything is okay, he will come out, followed by the hen a few minutes later.

# Lories And Lorikeets

When breeding these birds (which should not create too many problems), they should be disturbed as little as possible. They can be nervous and will leave the nest very quickly if you get too close. In such cases, eggs may be damaged or young may even be accidentally dragged out of the nest and dropped on the floor, with disastrous consequences.

## Genus *Psitteuteles* (Green Lories)

This genus of mainly green colored, small, and aggressive lories contains just two species that occur in the mountains of northern Australia and New Guinea. The diet consists of nectar, pollen, small insects, and fruits, but also much unripe and ripe grass and weed seeds. The voice is high and shrill. The varied or red-crowned lorikeet (*P. versicolor*) comes from Australia, where it is legally protected and may not be shot or taken. This bird may not be exported, so only smuggled (the act of bird smuggling must be condemned) specimens occasionally turn up.

## Goldie's Lorikeet—*P. goldiei*

**Distribution:** Found in the Weyland Mountains to southeastern Papua (New Guinea).

**Description:** It is predominently grass green with a yellow-green neck and underwing coverts. The lower body is also light yellow-green with dark green longitudinal stripes. The forehead and cheeks are respectively light red and violet colored; thus the Germans and the Dutch call the birds respectively Veilchenlori and Viooltjes lori! The tail is olive-green above and olive-yellow below. The beak is black, the iris is brown, and the feet are gray.

**Length:** 7.5 inches (19 cm); wings, 4.3 inches (11 cm); tail, 3 inches (7.5 cm). Juveniles are

Goldie's lorikeet is a willing breeder. The male is known for his amusing display. Various pairs can be housed in aviaries.

somewhat duller in color, but are still very similar to the adults.

**Habitat:** This attractive bird, discovered by a certain Goldie during an expedition to the Astrolable Mountains, occurs in pairs and small groups; youngsters get together in larger groups to forage in the treetops. The species occurs to an altitude of 9190 feet (2800 m). The diet is pollen nectar, insects, and soft fruit.

**Aviculture:** This species first arrived in the United States (Chicago Zoo) in 1949, and has been available in Europe since 1950. It will do well on the normal lory diet (see page 25). I have also noticed that various hummingbird menus available in the trade can be given as a treat; I have found this to be loved by all of the smaller lorikeets and is good for a change now and again. Although this species is a little shy at first and will spend hours in the nest box, they soon

# Lories And Lorikeets

will become reasonably tame and trusting once settled.

I have several pairs and none of them seem to mind when I look in the nest box, even when the hen is sitting on eggs or youngsters! The cock often keeps company with his brooding mate or sits close to the nest. When I offer fresh food the cock always eats first, followed by the hen after a few minutes. Sometimes the hen spends a longer period in the nest and the birds keep in contact by calling. The incubation period is 20 to 21 days; the eggs measure about $15/16$ by $53/64$ inch (24 x 21 mm). Both parents feed the young, but the male is markedly more active in this task than the hen. At three weeks of age, the young open their eyes. Due to the very fluid droppings, it is recommended that the nest bedding is renewed at least twice a week—that is after the young are 10 to 12 days old and have a good "droppings production!" Both adults and young soon get used to this activity and I have never lost any young due to it. The young leave the nest at about 6 weeks of age, but they are fed, especially by the cock, for some time thereafter. At this time, the hen is often starting on her next brood. I leg band the young when they are about nine to ten days old, using an $11/64$-inch (4.5-mm) diameter ring. The juveniles get their purple-red crown at about four months and are almost indistinguishable from the adults at eight months.

These lories, fortunately, are regularly propagated and it should not be too difficult to obtain good unrelated breeding pairs. They are bred often in room aviaries and large cages, so a large outdoor aviary is, in this case, not essential. The species is thus suited to those fanciers with minimal space, giving them the opportunity to view the birds at close quarters, and to regularly propagate them. It has also been ascertained that birds that are given regular supplies of willow or fruit tree twigs, will leave the wooden cage or aviary framework undamaged (or almost undamaged).

The birds should be brought indoors for the winter unless they have a lightly heated night shelter. They should be kept at least at room temperature. Although they come from high altitudes in the wild, they are very intolerant of our cold winters. In the wild they usually descend to lower altitudes for the night.

## Genus *Trichoglossus* (Wedge-tailed Lories)

There are eight species and more than 30 subspecies recognized in this genus. They have a characteristically slender body form, a long wedge-shaped tail, and an incurving upper mandible. On the wing, they keep in contact by their continual communication calls. The dominant colors are green, yellow, blue, and red. The best known member of the genus is the rainbow or green-naped lory (*T. h. haemadotus*) with some 22 subspecies! Food consists mainly of pollen and nectar, but also, as I have observed in the wild birds, insects and their larvae, soft, sweet fruits (especially berries), and half-ripe grass and weed seeds.

Most species in the genus can be kept in a minimum 5-foot (1.5-m) long aviary. In the colder states, they are mostly kept in indoor aviaries; as long as normal room temperature is maintained there are no problems. A garden aviary must have a night shelter, where the nest/sleep box is placed as high up as possible. A 1.2-inch (3-cm) layer of wood pulp should be placed in the floor of the nest box; keep an eye on this "upholstery" and it should be replaced if it gets wet from the copious fluid droppings. The hen lays two to three eggs (depending on the species) that hatch after 23 to 28 days. The young fledge at six to ten weeks, but are fed by the adults, especially the cock, for a further two to three weeks. Prior to fledging you

# *Lories And Lorikeets*

should see that the aviary wire is shielded with willow and fruit tree twigs, with leaves, so that the shy and nervous young do not injure themselves by flying into the wire. In the third or fourth week after fledging, the cock is likely to start assaulting his offspring and will injure them unless you remove them to their own aviary; do not forget to place the above mentioned twigs in the aviary.

Some species will do reasonably well in a cage, though I am no great supporter of this! I have seen many really tame specimens that could even talk a little. I would recommended that caged specimens get a daily "flight" in the room, but due to the fluid droppings of these birds one cannot really consider them good household companions! The following species has been renamed several times and was once in *Glossopsitta*, then *Psitteuteles*; in older books they may still be found under these genera.

## Iris Lorikeet — *Trichoglossus iris iris*

**Distribution:** Found in Timor and Wetar (Indonesia).

**Description:** Ground color is pale green. The breast is light green with a horizontal dark green scalloped pattern; the back and wings are dark green. The underside of the tail and the neck band are yellow-green; the forehead and the crown are purple-red, the back of the head is light green with a hazy red scalloping. There is a purple, oval patch behind the eye. The beak is orange-red, with small red flecks on the lower mandible; the iris is orange-red, the feet are gray. Cock and hen are similar in appearance. The colors and patterns may vary slightly from one individual to the next. Fledglings are duller in color and the red on the head especially is only vaguely discernible.

**Length:** 8 inches (20 cm); wings, 4.5 inches (11.5 cm); tail, 3 inches (7.5 cm).

**Habitat:** Unfortunately little is known about the wild habits of this somewhat vulnerable spe-

cies. I have seen them to be quite abundant in western Timor; especially in the mountains, where they operate in small groups and keep in close contact when on the wing. They occur to an altitude of 1500 m.

**Aviculture:** The first specimens in Europe were shown in the Berlin Zoo in 1932. The first captive breeding reports came from the San Diego Zoo. With a good breeding pair they are not difficult to breed. The hen lays two eggs that are incubated for 23 days. The young leave the nest at 23 days. A colleague, F. Beswerda, from the Netherlands is one of the best known breeders of this species and he wrote me the following: "I was lucky to be able to obtain two of these little lories in 1979. As I could find no concrete guidelines on sex determination anywhere in the literature, I

Left: the iris lorikeet; right: Meyer's lorikeet. Both species are attractive small parrots that have been readily available recently. They are fairly prolific and thrive well in small aviaries.

# Lories And Lorikeets

had no idea whether these birds were a true pair. According to Forshaw (*Parrots of the World*) the hen should have a brown iris, while in the cock this should be orange-red. In my two birds this was not the case; they both had orange-red irises and as they did not seem to be particularly interested in each other I assumed I had two cocks. After about 18 months of searching at home and abroad, I came in contact with a fancier who had a single bird that, according to him, was a hen and this bird came into my possession. Placing the three birds together in a cage, I could still see no difference in eye color, so that I now thought I was the owner of three cocks! This was especially so, as I had carried out the pelvic test as one would with lovebirds and could find little space between the pubic bones in any of the birds. As these were some of the most attractive birds in my collection, I had no immediate thoughts of getting rid of them and I began another "town and country" search, hoping to find more examples, but without success.

The three birds were placed in a room aviary approximately 3 by 3 by 6 feet (1 by 1 by 1.8 m) in width, depth, and height and given a sleep/nest box approximatley 8 by 8 by 11 inches (20 x 20 x 28 cm) in which they all slept. The birds lived happily and twitteringly together in the aviary for several months, without any apparent discord.

As I was still under the impression that I possessed three males, I did not regularly inspect the nest box. One day as all of the birds were out of the box I had a quick look inside and, to my astonishment, and joy, there were two eggs in the nest! Closer inspection revealed the eggs to be probably fertile. The two eggs hatched after a certain time but I was, of course, unable to say what the exact incubation time was. The young were fed by all three adults, which was good; it meant that these were youngsters with three parents!

I was now sure that I had at least one hen in my possession, but I had no idea which two were the father and mother of the young. I thus took it for granted that I had one hen and two cocks but, as it turned out, I was still wrong! About two months after the first young had fledged, there were suddenly four more eggs in the nest! As I knew that this species laid only two eggs per clutch, I could only assume that two hens had laid. After another pelvic test I discovered that indeed, two of the birds had a .4-inch (1-cm) space between the pubic bones while the third had hardly any space at all.

Three young hatched from the four eggs; the fourth egg was damaged during the incubation, which was carried out by both hens. These three young were also exemplarily reared by all three adults. I am now the proud owner of eight iris lories; probably at this time the only examples of the species in our country."

## Meyer's Lorikeet —
### *T. flavoviridis meyeri*
**Distribution:** Found in Celebes (Indonesia).

**Description:** Predominantly dark green with yellow flecks here and there. The head is brownish-black with yellow cheek patches. The breast and belly are yellow-green checkered. There is a naked, gray eye-ring. The beak is orange, the iris is reddish-brown, and the feet are gray. The hen is usually less intensively colored than the cock, especially with regard to the cheek patches. Fledglings resemble the hen, with vague belly markings and a darker beak.

**Length:** 6.7 inches (17 cm); wings, 4 inches (10 cm); tail, 2.8 inches (7 cm).

**Habitat:** These small, somewhat plain lories, occur in groups of 40 or so birds in the wild, frequently in the company of ornate lories (see page 81), to an altitude of 6560 feet (2000 m). They have a shrill, penetrating voice.

**Aviculture:** Birds in good feed and condition show off the contrast well between the light green breast checkering and the cheek patch, against the dark-green ground color of the rest of the body. It is a shame that this pretty bird is not more frequently imported as it does not demand a great deal of space; it will do well even in a cage 32 by 39 by 24 inches (80 x 100 x 60 cm). In addition to the usual lory diet, it should be given a daily treat of a teaspoonful of black or striped sunflower seeds, millet, or hemp. They simply love millet spray, as well as soft fruit (apples and berries). The hen incubates her two eggs for 23 days. They cannot tolerate cold and should be kept indoors at a minimum temperature of 54°F (12°C ) during the winter.

## Ornate Lory — *T. ornatus*

**Distribution:** Found in Celebes and the outlying islands (Indonesia).

**Description:** The back and wings are dark green, the crown is purplish-blue, the neck band is yellow, broken by the green of the back. There is a purplish-blue cheek patch, which runs from the eye to the neck band. The breast is purple-red with blue transverse stripes; the belly and thighs are green with yellow stripes. The beak is red and the iris is reddish. The naked eye-ring is gray, as are the feet.

**Length:** 9.5 (24 cm); wings, 5.1 inches (13 cm); tail, 2.8 to 3.1 inches (7–8 cm). The young birds are duller in color with a darker beak.

**Habitat:** These are common birds that occur in pairs or small groups to an altitude of 3300 feet (1000 m), frequently in the company of Meyer's lorikeets (see page 80). The food is largely fruits, nectar, pollen, and insects. Some seeds, especially of *Tectona* and *Casuarina* (Forshaw/Low) are also taken. The birds have a fast flight, are far from shy, and come frequently in the neighborhood of settlements in the hills and valleys. The hen lays two eggs, about 0.8 by 0.9 inch (21.1 x 21.7 mm), in a hollow limb high in a tree. Incubation takes about 27 days and the young leave the

nest at 11 weeks. They are fed by the parents for a further couple of weeks and return to the nest to sleep at night, as the adults do all year-round (the cock even spending the night with the hen when she is incubating). Once independent, the young form into large groups. In Celebes, the birds are popular as household pets! They are hand-reared with corn and mashed banana.

**Aviculture:** The first birds arrived in Europe in (England) in 1873, and the first documented breeding took place in France during 1883. Recent breeding results are disappointing, probably due partly to the fact that it is difficult to form true pairs of this species as there are no visible sex differences. The same can be said about the following (*T. haematodus*) species. This species has a harsh voice, which is surprising as it is not one of the more robust lories! During the winter months, the birds must be kept in a warm indoor or heated outdoor aviary.

## Green-naped Lory — *T. h. haematodus*

**Synonym:** Rainbow Lory

**Distribution:** Found in Buru, Amboina, Ceram, Ceramlaunt, Goram, Watubela, and western Papua; also the islands in Geelvink Bay (with the exception of Biak), and western New Guinea.

**Description:** The back and wings are dark green; the belly also is dark green, but with a dark blue wash; the head is purple-blue, the breast is light red with blue-black transverse stripes. The thighs are yellow-green striped. The beak is orange-red, the iris is reddish-brown, and the feet are gray.

**Length:** 11 inches (28 cm); wings, 5.5 inches (14 cm); tail, 4.3 inches (11 cm).

**Habitat:** It is remarkable that so little is known about the wild habits of such a common and widespread species as this. It occurs in thick woodland and lives on pollen, nectar, soft fruits, and unripe grass and weed seeds. I have observed these birds in New Guinea towards evening when they gather in large groups to go to their communal roost. It is usually deep in the night before peace reigns at these roosts as the birds are continually squabbling for the best perches!

**Aviculture:** One of the best known and loved, and easy to breed lories, they have been kept in Europe since 1872! In the breeding season the birds become quite aggressive, and each pair must have its own aviary with night shelter (where the thick-walled sleep/nest box is affixed). The sexes can be determined accurately only by endoscopy or blood test (see page 31). The hen lays two eggs, about 1 by 0.9 inch (26 x 22 mm), that are incubated for 27 days. The white-downed youngsters grow quickly and in ten days they grow a thicker, gray-colored down. The eyes open at two weeks and the first feathers appear at about one month. They fledge at about two months but return there to sleep at night. They are fed for about two more weeks by their parents, although they quickly learn to eat fruit or lory food themselves. Once independent, the young must be removed to separate accommodations as the parents will become aggressive, especially if they want to start a new family. It is essential to shield the nervous young birds from the aviary wire by affixing willow or fruit tree twigs; this will help prevent injury. All *haematodus* lories like plenty of space, thus the larger the flight the more contented the birds will be. During the winter months, they must be brought indoors or have the benefit of a heated night shelter. They should have a thick-walled box in which to sleep at night. I use the following sleep/nest box measurements for all *haematodus:* 10 by 10 by 18 inches (25 x 25 x 45 cm).

**Subspecies:** These are often available, breed fairly readily, and all require similar avicultural care to the nominate form.

1.  **Mitchell's or red-breasted lorikeet** *(T. h. mitchelli)* from Bali and Lombok (Indonesia). The cock has an almost completely red upper breast, whereas in the hen, the feathers are yellow

edged. The abdomen is dark purple to black. The head is reddish-brown, the cheeks are greenish, and the neck band (nuchal band) is greenish-yellow. **Length:** 9.4 inches (24 cm); wings, 5.1 inches (13 cm); tail, 4 inches (10 cm). This subspecies is difficult to distinguish from the next described, and to make things worse it seems that the two subspecies frequently interbreed in the wild.

2.  **Forsten's Lorikeet** *(T. h. forsteni)* from Sumbawa (Indonesia), but I also saw them on Bali and Lombok! The upper breast is scarlet, the abdomen is purple or dark mauve. The dark purplish head has violet-blue stripes. There is a dark purple patch on the yellowish-green neck. **Length:** 10.6 inches (27 cm); wings, 5.3 (13.5 cm); tail, 4 inches (10 cm).

Mitchell's lorikeet inhabits Bali and Lombok (Indonesia) and has a scarlet breast with green, yellow, or bluish edges to the feathers.

# Lories And Lorikeets

3. **Edward's Lorikeet** (*T. h. capistratus*) from Timor (Indonesia). This subspecies has a yellow upper breast; each feather is tipped with red. The neck band is yellow; the abdomen is very dark mauve. There are conspicuous blue stripes on the brown head (these have a violet sheen in certain lights). The cheeks are blue. **Length:** 10.6 (27 cm); wings, 5.7 inches (14.5 cm); tail, 4.5 inches (11.5 cm). With sufficient comparative material, the sexes are relatively easy to distinguish; the cock is generally more robust than the hen and usually has more orange in the yellow breast. These birds have been found to be relatively shy and some tend to stay so for years; disappearing into their nest box at the slightest disturbance! However, they are not particularly difficult to breed, especially if the nest box is "hidden" behind plenty of twigs. I can recommend this subspecies for beginners if they are prepared to accept the birds' shyness. Do not confuse this bird with the *T. h. moluccanus*, which has a blue belly, rather than green.

4. **Weber's Lorikeet** (*T. h. weberi*) from Flores (Indonesia) has a greenish-yellow neck band. The head is dark green with lighter stripes. Some of the forehead feathers are blue-tipped. The upper breast is the same color as that of the Mitchell's lorikeet, but it also has a scattering of dark green feathers throughout; the same green occurs on the abdomen. **Length:** 8.5 inches (21.5 cm); wings, 5 inches (12.5 cm); tail, 3.7 inches (9.5 cm).

5. **Massena's or Coconut Lorikeet** (*T. h. massena*) from the Bismarck Archipelago, via the Solomon Islands to New Hebrides. The nape is brown and the abdomen is dark green ending in greenish-yellow. The upper breast is reddish with small black feathertips. The neck band is yellowish-green and the head is dark blue. The back of the head and the cheeks are black. The ear coverts are dark blue. **Length:** 12 inches (29.5 cm); wings, 5.5 inches (14 cm); tail, 4.4 inches (11.2 cm).

6. **Deplanche's Lorikeet** (*T. h. deplanchii*) from New Caledonia and the Loyalty Islands. This subspecies has less brown in the nape than the preceding bird. The nuchal band is yellow. The upper breast is similar to that of the foregoing subspecies. The head is a deep blue. **Length:** 11.4 inches (29 cm); wings, 5.7 inches (14.5 cm); tail, 4.1 inches (10.5 cm).

7. **Swainson's, Blue Mountain, or Rainbow Lorikeet** (*T. h. moluccanus*) from the eastern parts of Australia, Tasmania, Kangaroo Island, and the Eyre Peninsula. The abdomen is a rich violet; the breast is red with yellow; the nuchal band is greenish-yellow. The feather shafts can be seen clearly on the violet colored head. **Length:** 11.4 inches (29 cm); wings, 6 inches (15 cm); tail, 5.3 inches (13.5 cm).

Swainson's (also known as rainbow) lorikeet was the first Australian parrot to be described and illustrated in Brown's *New Illustrations of Zoology* (1774). A true pair indulges in amusing antics.

# Lories And Lorikeets

8. **Red-collared Lorikeet** (*T. h. rubritorquis*) from northern Australia and Melville Island, has a dark green abdomen, an orange-red nuchal band and upper breast, and a blue head and throat. **Length:** 11.4 inches (29 cm); wings, 6 inches (15 cm); tail, 5.3 inches (13.5 cm).

## Perfect Lory—*T. euteles*

**Synonyms:** Yellow-headed or Plain Lorikeet

**Distribution:** Found in the Lesser Sunda Islands and Timor.

**Description:** The main coloring is light green, but the head and the whole underside are yellow to olive-green. The outer tail feathers are yellow-edged beneath. The beak is orange, the iris is red and the feet are gray. There is a naked gray eyering.

**Length:** 9 inches (23 cm); wings, 5.1 inches (13 cm); tail, 4 inches (10 cm). Juveniles are duller in color and the head is greener.

**Habitat:** These somewhat plain green birds are pronounced forest dwellers, and not much is known about their wild habits. I have observed them in small to large groups (up to 100 birds) high in the treetops. They occur up to an altitude of 8200 feet (2500 m) and feed on the usual lory menu. Their flight is fast and they hold contact with their shrill calls.

**Aviculture:** The first examples were introduced to the public in the London Zoo in 1896. According to T. Pagel, the San Diego Zoo was rather successful in breeding about 40 young between 1942 and 1972! The hen lays three to four (!) eggs, about 1.0 by 0.9 inch (24.4 x 22.8 mm), and the incubation time is 23 to 25 days. With relatively more young than most lories it is essential to keep the bottom of the nest box dry from the copious fluid droppings by regularly changing the 1.2-inch (3-cm) layer of wood pulp. The young leave the nest at about two months of age, but continue to sleep there at night. After two more weeks, the young are best moved to separate quarters in order to avoid mishaps. The cock especially can get very aggressive, with sometimes fatal results.

## Genus *Pseudeos* (White-rumped Lories)

This is a monotypic genus and many ornithologists consider it to be a link between the genera *Eos* and *Trichoglossus*. The bird has a rounded tail that is shorter than in the *Trichoglossus* species. The body is also somewhat more strongly built. There is a naked patch, orange in color, just below the lower mandible. This unfeathered patch is shared only with the genus *Chalcopsitta* (see page 86), but in the latter it is black. There is no obvious sexual dimorphism. The courtship procedure is quite interesting, the cock emitting whispering and growling noises as he flutters his wings and bows, stretching his neck in front of the hen. Copulation takes a relatively long time. As with many parrotlike birds (especially those from Australia), the cock places one foot on the hen's back and holds himself securely on the perch with the other.

## Dusky Lory—*P. fuscata*

**Distribution:** Found in New Guinea, Salawati, western Papuan Islands, and Japan Island (in the Geelvink Bay).

**Description:** The total first impressions of this bird's coloring is a fairly uniform brownish-black, but on closer inspection its diverse coloration becomes apparent. Most conspicuous are the orange-red bands of which one runs across the throat, the other across the breast and upper belly. The large underwing coverts and the base of the inside of each primary wing feather are also orange colored. The breast feathers are edged in gray; the rump is all white; the tail feathers are vi-

84

# *Lories And Lorikeets*

The dusky lory is an excellent talker as well as a hardy and fairly consistent breeder, although aggressive when sitting on the eggs. These highly intelligent birds have somewhat shrill voices.

olet-brown, yellowish beneath, and orange-red, at the roots beneath.

**Length:** 9.6 to 10.2 inches (24.5–26 cm); wings, 6.2 to 6.5 inches (15.5–16.5 cm); tail, 3.1 to 3.3 inches (8–8.5 cm). In juveniles the orange-red parts are sometimes more yellowish, but it is usually difficult to distinguish them from the parents. The rump is yellowish-white and the beak is dark.

**Habitat:** These birds are active to an altitude of 6560 feet (2000 m), usually in savannah and open woodland. They occur in groups of 20 to 100 individuals, but after the breeding season I have seen flocks of several hundreds in flight. Their food consists of pollen, nectar, fruits (mainly berries), and small insects. The birds are very noisy and their shrill communication calls can be heard from some distance away.

**Aviculture:** The first specimens arrived in the London Zoo in 1909, and they were also to be seen in the Berlin Zoo a year later. Dr. E. Hopkins was the first successful United States breeder and successfully bred them in 1940. Dusky lories are today regularly available on the market. They soon become tame and trusting toward their keeper, but pairs should not be kept together with other parrotlike birds including members of their own species in the relatively small confines of an aviary. The sleep/nest box 11¾ by 11¾ by 15¾ inches (30 x 30 x 40 cm) must have a good layer of absorbent material in the base. The hen lays two eggs, about 1 by 0.9 inch (27.8 x 24.1mm), with an interval of about 24 hours between. The incubation time is about 26 days. The young are only sparsely covered with white down for the first few days, but after a week they have a thick gray coat of down. The eyes open at 14 to 16 days and the young leave the nest at about seven weeks. The adults continue to feed them for another 18 to 22 days, but after this they must be moved to another aviary. T. Pagel reports that a German breeder, R. Bruch, had a pair that laid three eggs in a clutch; all three eggs hatched and the young were all successfully reared. Personally, I like to leg band the young when they are about four weeks old, with a ⁹⁄₃₂-inch (7-mm) band. At seven months of age, the young are fully colored and indistinguishable from the adults.

One concluding note: the literature frequently states that there is recognizable sexual dimorphism in this species, but I would dispute this, especially as the so-called differences are not always visible. However, I must report that three of my pairs showed a similar difference between cock and hen: in the cock the upper part of the tail feather is reddish-brown, whereas in the hen, this is dark blue.

# *Lories And Lorikeets*

## Genus *Chalcopsitta* (Glossy Lories)

There are four species and nine subspecies recognized in this genus. Like the foregoing genus, there is a typical naked throat spot, but here it is colored black. There is a black colored naked eyering. The tail is long and rounded. The neck feathers and the feathers at the back of the head are especially narrow and pointed. All members of this genus are extremely aggressive toward all other birds, but a pair kept in a roomy aviary with a heated night shelter soon will become tame and trusting toward their owner. The shrill, piercing call that they will use frequently at first, will be heard less and less as the birds settle.

## Duivenbode's Lory—*C. duivenbodei duivenbodei*

**Distribution:** Found in northern parts of western New Guinea from Geelvink Bay to the Aitape area.

**Description:** The main color is predominantly dark brown; the head is brownish-black, the forehead and part of the crown are yellow. The whole head and neck are covered with longitudinal gold-colored stripes; the thigh feathers are golden; small yellow feathers are also sprinkled about the body. The tail is yellow beneath, gold-brown above; the underwing coverts are also yellow, the primaries are brownish-black with large light yellow patches. The beak is black, the iris is reddish-brown, and the feet are dark gray.

**Length:** 12.2 inches (31 cm); wings, 6.9 inches (17.5 cm); tail, 5.3 inches (13.5 cm).

**Habitat:** Not uncommon in the wild, this species occurs in the lowlands, in groups of six to ten individuals. They hold continual contact with each other with their shrill calls. They spend most of the day high in the treetops. Unfortunately not much is known about the wild habits of these birds.

**Aviculture:** This unusually colored lory species was first exhibited in the London Zoo in 1929. At the present time, the bird is being bred regularly both in bird gardens and by private aviculturists. It requires the normal lory diet (see page 25), fresh, sweet fruit (apple, berries), unripe corncobs, and boiled rice.

At first sight, these birds do not seem to be particularly attractively colored. But once carefully acclimatized and brought into good condition, you will be pleased with the unusual colors, especially when they spread their wings to show the golden-yellow undersides that are in stark contrast to the mainly brown plumage. It is important to acclimatize these birds with the greatest of care, as many newly imported birds unfortunately (and unnecessarily!) die when they get into inexperienced hands. As noted earlier, they must not be kept at less than normal room temperature as they are not very cold tolerant.

Duivenbode lory is a hardy bird, rather aggressive when nesting but nevertheless one of the best pets known.

# Lories And Lorikeets

## Black Lory — *C. atra atra*

**Distribution**: Found in West Irian, the islands of Batanta and Salawati, and western New Guinea (especially western Vogelkop).

**Description:** The whole body is black with a purplish sheen; the rump is blue, the ventral region and underside of the tail has an orange-yellow wash that runs into yellow. The beak is black, the iris is reddish-brown and the feet also are black.

**Length:** 13 inches (32.5 cm); wings, 7.3 inches (18.5 cm); tail, 5.1 inches (13 cm). The young have a lighter-colored throat patch (see genus), and the eye-ring is also lighter in tint; the iris is dark.

**Habitat:** The birds are found mainly along the margins of forests or in isolated pockets of trees in the savannah. They operate in groups of 18 to 24 individuals. They feed especially on the pollen and nectar of palms and eucalyptus trees. They have a remarkably strong call, which they use fully as they fly over open areas.

**Aviculture:** This species was first shown in England in 1904. It will do well on the usual lory diet (see page 25), but extra fruit must be offered; apple, berries, sultanas, figs, and papaya. A good canary rearing food (CéDé or L/M's Universal Plus) also will be accepted eagerly. As the toenails tend to grow long and sharp, it is recommended that a variety of rough-barked natural twigs are offered as perches. A daily bath of fresh water must be available; they also love to take a shower in the summer rainfall. The hen lays two eggs, about 1.2 by 1 inch (31 x 25.7 mm), which hatch after about 25 days. The young leave the nest at two months of age.

Newly imported birds are frequently in bad condition, and only experienced aviculturists should attempt to carefully acclimatize them. Once accustomed to the new climate and diet, however, they are quite robust birds that will do well in an aviary spacious enough for them to put in a bit of serious flying (this goes for all members of this genus!). This species is usually sexually mature in its third year; in any case it should not be bred before then. Breeding too early may result in weak youngsters, or the parents will not look after them properly or even abandon them. The sleep/nest box should be well protected from the elements in a well-built night shelter.

## Yellow-streaked Lory — *C. sintillata, sintillata*

**Distribution:** Found in New Guinea from Triton Bay to the Fly River.

**Description:** It is mainly dark green; the head is brownish-black, and the forehead and part of the crown are red. The whole body is covered with longitudinal gold-colored stripes. The thigh feathers are red, and small red feathers are spread

The yellow-streaked lory is a delightful bird, but tends to be loud and shrill!

87

# *Lories And Lorikeets*

Little lorikeet (Glossopsitta pusilla). This largely green-colored species with red cheeks and forehead, native of southeastern Austrailia and Tasmania, is a tiny jewel under the lories. The hen lays 2 to 5 eggs.

throughout the plumage. The tail feathers are red beneath, running into gold-brown towards the tips; the underwing coverts are also red; the primaries are brownish-black with large light yellow patches. The beak is black, the iris is reddish-orange, and the feet are gray.

**Length:** 11.8 inches (30 cm); wings, 6.7 inches (17 cm); tail, 4.1 inches (10.5 cm).

**Habitat:** This interesting bird is an inhabitant mainly of the lowlands where it lives in groups of 26 to 30 individuals along the forest margins or among groves of trees in more open country. They frequently fly in great arcs, screaming loudly as they again swoop down to the treetops in search of pollen, nectar, small insects, and fruits. They can be quite a pest in coconut plantations!

**Aviculture:** This species is—at least from this genus—the best known, most widely kept lory. They are generally, especially after careful acclimatization, strong in constitution. They were first introduced to the public at the London Zoo in 1872. The hen lays two eggs in a clutch and these are incubated for 25 to 27 days. The young leave the nest at about 12 weeks of age. With optimum care, these birds show a sheen in their plumage that is seldom seen in other lories or lorikeets. I find them exceedingly sportive and excellent fliers—thus they should have an aviary with a flight at least 10 feet (3 m) long—when the bright red and yellow of the underwings shows up in great contrast to the green of the other plumage. With good care they soon become very tame and trusting toward their keeper. They sometimes can be aggressive to strangers and I would not recommend you take a stranger *in* the aviary with you! Even when you approach the aviary with a stranger, the birds will angrily fluff their feathers and scream loudly. They do really well on the normal lory diet (see page 25), and as a treat can be given unripe corncobs, and boiled rice with honey. I would recommend that the birds are kept at not less than room temperature in the winter months.

88

# Useful Literature and Addresses

## Books

Forshaw, Joseph M. *Australian Parrots*, 2nd edition. Lansdowne, Melbourne, Australia, 1989.
— — *Parrots of the World*, 3rd edition. Lansdowne, Melbourne, Australia, 1989.
Low, Rosemary. *The Complete Book of Parrots*. Barron's Educational Series, Inc., Hauppauge, New York, 1989.
— — *Parrots: Their Care and Breeding*, 3rd edition. Blanford Press, London, New York, Sydney, 1992.
— — *Lories and Lorikeets*, 2nd unrevised edition (first edition, 1977). TFH Publications, Inc., Neptune, New Jersey, 1991.
Munro Doane, Bonnie. *The Parrot in Health and Illness*. Howell, New York, 1991.
Silva, Tony. *Psittaculture, The Breeding, Rearing and Management of Parrots*. Silvio Mattachione & Co., Pickering, Ontario, Canada, 1991.
Vanderhoof, John. *Lories and Lorikeets in Aviculture*. Woodlake, California, 1990.
Vriends, Matthew M. *Simon & Schuster's Guide to Pet Birds*, 6th edition. Simon & Schuster, New York, 1992.
— — *The New Bird Handbook*. Barron's Educational Series, Inc., Hauppauge, New York, 1989.

## Magazines

*AFA Watchbird*
(American Federation of Aviculture)
  Box 56218
  Phoenix, Arizona 85079-6218

*American Cage Bird Magazine*
  1 Glamore Court
  Smithtown, New York 11787

*Journal of the Association of Avian Veterinarians*
  5770 Lake Worth Road
  Lake Worth, Florida 33463-3299

*Lory Journal International*
  c/o Mr. Jos Hubers
  Klein Baal 33
  6685 AC Haalderen
  The Netherlands
  (quarterly magazine, printed in English, Dutch, and German)

*Parrotworld*
(National Parrot Association)
  8 North Hoffman Lane
  Hauppauge, New York 11788

## Aviculture Societies
### Canada
British Columbia Avicultural Society
  11784-9th Avenue
  North Delta, British Columbia V4C 3H6

The Canadian Avicultural Society
  32 Dronmore Court
  Willowdale, Ontario M2R 2H5

Canadian Parrot Association
  Pine Oaks R.R. #3
  St. Catharines, Ontario L2R 6P9

### Great Britain
The Avicultural Society
  The Secretary
  Warren Hill, Halford's Lane
  Hartley Wintney, Hampshire RG27 8AG

# Useful Literature and Addresses

The European Aviculture Council
c/o Mr. Dave Axtell
P.O. Box 74
Bury St. Edmunds, Suffolk IP30 OHS

## United States

American Federation of Aviculture (AFA)
P.O. Box 56218
Phoenix, Arizona 85079-6218

Association of Avian Veterinarians
5770 Lake Worth Road
Lake Worth, Florida 33463-3299

Avicultural Society of America, Inc.
P.O. Box 2196
Redondo Beach, California 90218

International Loriidae Society
17704 S. Tapps Drive East
Summer, Washington 98390-9172

National Parrot Association
8 North Hoffman Lane
Hauppauge, New York 11788

The Society of Parrot Breeders and Exhibitors
P.O. Box 369
Groton, Massachusetts 01450

# *Index*

Page references in **boldface** indicate color photos. **C1** indicates front cover; **C2**, inside front cover; **C3**, inside back cover; **C4**, back cover.

# Index

# *Index*